The Aboriginals

The Faces of Australia Series consists of records and cassettes, together with companion books, giving a comprehensive and entertaining history of Australia and its people in musical and literary form. For details concerning the series write to:
Ted Egan, PO Box 1694 Alice Springs 5750, NT, Australia

First published in 1987 by
Greenhouse Publications Pty Ltd
385-387 Bridge Road
Richmond 3121, Victoria, Australia

© In this collection, Ted Egan 1987

Typeset in Australia by Trade Graphics Pty Ltd
Printed and bound in Australia by Impact Printing

National Library of Australia
Cataloguing-in-Publication data:

The Aboriginals songbook.
  ISBN 0 864 36 079 7.

  (1). Aborigines, Australian—Music. (2). Aboriginal
  Australian songs. I. Egan, Ted.

784.7'69915

Distributed in Australia by Gordon and Gotch Limited
Brisbane, Sydney, Melbourne, Adelaide, Perth, Launceston

Distributed in New Zealand by Golden Press

The Aboriginals

SONGBOOK

Compiled by Ted Egan

GREENHOUSE PUBLICATIONS

Foreword by Lowitja (Lois) O'Donoghue
Musical notation by Erik Kowarski
Cover illustration by Elizabeth Durack

Ted Egan

Ted Egan went to the Northern Territory of Australia at age seventeen, intending to spend three months in Darwin and then travel to South America to be a cowboy. Over thirty years later he still hasn't made it to South America. He now lives in Alice Springs and his principal interest is in collecting and recording the history of frontier Australia. He writes, sings and records his own songs, and regularly features these songs in the Ted Egan Outback Show in Alice Springs.

His early, and continuing contacts with Aboriginal people have given him a deep insight into their unique occupancy of this harsh, uncompromising yet starkly beautiful continent. He speaks two Aboriginal dialects, and has conducted Aboriginal Studies courses, mainly for urbanised Aboriginal children, at the Alice Springs High School.

His music is clearly influenced by his Aboriginal contacts and his Celtic ancestors, the first to come to Australia being a Cornishman to Portland, Victoria, in 1840. Despite the fact that the last Celt in his family was an Irish-born farmer named Peter Brennan who came to Australia over a hundred years ago Ted Egan's songs bear the unmistakeable stamp of the Celts.

Ted Egan is a graduate of the Australian National University, and gained his Bachelor of Arts Degree the hard way, studying under kerosene lamps in the bush. He majored in Australian Studies and Politics. He is in the process of producing a series of record albums, with companion books, titled *The Faces of Australia Series*. The series is Ted Egan's interpretation of Australian history, in song and verse.

4

Foreword to the Series

Ted Egan's plan to release a series of record albums with accompanying books is one that should have the enthusiastic support of his wide range of listeners.

The records and tapes he has already produced give a moving and multi-sided picture of the opening up of the vast inland of this continent. His songs are not only entertaining, they are also of considerable educational significance and arouse in all age groups an interest in, and an appreciation of, the men and women who pioneered our 'great Australian loneliness'. His repertoire is a subtle mingling of the romance, pathos and humour of our unique Australian heritage.

I have therefore, no hesitation in recommending wholeheartedly support for this project and I have every confidence that it will be of great popular appeal.

MARY DURACK
PERTH

W.A. Newspapers

Foreword

Ted Egan's decision to release a book and album entitled *The Aboriginals* is most appropriate and timely as we approach 1988, our Bicentennial year, because it is a sincere attempt to put into perspective the history of my people.

I am pleased to have been invited to make comment because I know from personal experience the heartache of being removed from my mother at the age of two, and have suffered the traumas resulting from the many misguided policies of various governments.

In growing up, I was led to believe that my Aboriginal heritage was unacceptable and something to be ashamed of. It wasn't until I was thirty that my nursing career took me to the north-west of South Australia, where I first met my mother. I found I was part of a great new family, with a language I couldn't speak, that my real name was Lowitja and that I belonged to a piece of land near Indulkana. That meeting brought about a greater awareness of my real identity, and my life took on a new direction, which has enabled me to influence policies affecting my people.

Ted correctly leads the reader to the conclusion that heritage, land and identity are the essential elements in giving meaning and a proper place in society and I believe many will be moved to join in this search for a better life for all as a result of reading this book.

Thank you Ted for a job well done.

Lowitja

LOWITJA (LOIS) O'DONOGHUE CBE, AM
AUSTRALIAN OF THE YEAR 1984

Contents

Acknowledgements

The author wishes to thank the following:

The many Aboriginal people who have given me insights into Australia I would not otherwise have received.

The musicians and singers who participated in the companion L.P. album *The Aboriginals*.

Elizabeth Durack for permission to use her painting *Stockman Biddy: The Drover's Boy* as front cover for the book and record.

Erik Kowarski for the musical notation in this book and for being Musical Director of the album; Hugh McDonald for assistance with production of the album.

Jeremy Long and Colin Tatz for invaluable assistance with research.

Peter Knight, Ernie Dingo and Bob Randall for permission to record and publish their songs *White Man, King Wally* and *Brown Skin Baby* respectively.

Dame Mary Durack for her Foreword to this book and for general support.

The descendants of Alyandabu for guidance which enabled me to write my song about her; and Robert Ingpen for his superb illustration based on an old photograph.

Allan Howard and the various other (acknowledged) sources of photographs.

Mentors Ted Evans, Bill Harney and Roger Jose who had a profound influence in my education about the Aboriginal people.

Lowitja (Lois) O'Donoghue for recording the linking commentary on the album.

Cover illustration

When Elizabeth Durack heard my song *The Drover's Boy* (included in *The Overlanders* book and album in this series) she shed a few tears. I asked her why. She replied that the song reminded her of Stockman Biddy. Stockman Biddy was one of the many Aboriginal women who made such a marvellous contribution to Australia's pastoral industry, working and dressing like men, and usually in the harshest of conditions. In the hope that the part played by these women will not be forgotten, or worse, ignored, I asked Elizabeth to paint Stockman Biddy as she might have looked as a young woman.

TED EGAN
ALICE SPRINGS, AUSTRALIA.

Aloysius Puantulura, the famous Tiwi dancer who led the contingent which danced the Royal Tour in 1954, is the most important Aboriginal person in my life

The Aboriginals are Australia's aborigines

In this book I shall use the word 'Aboriginal' as singular noun, 'Aboriginals' as plural noun, and 'Aboriginal' as adjective. There is a current quibble whether 'Aboriginals' is preferable to 'Aborigines' as plural noun: my thesis is that any original inhabitants of any country are 'aborigines' with a lower case 'a'. The requirement is for words to describe the particular group of people who have lived in Australia *ab origine* or 'from the beginning'.

Whatever nouns or adjectives are used to describe this particular group to the exclusion of all others should be dignified with a capital letter, as is the practice for all nationalities. My choice is that the Australian aborigines are best described categorically and distinctively as 'the Aboriginals'. Similarly, the aborigines of northern Canada are the Eskimos or the Inuits, the aborigines of northern Europe are the Lapps.

Fowler (Modern English Usage 1926) felt that to use 'aborigine' as either singular noun or adjective was 'anomalous and should be avoided' on the grounds that it was simply an amalgamation of the two Latin words *ab* and *origine*. Thus, while 'aborigines' as an English word derived from the Latin is a correct and allowable plural noun, it is not, in my opinion a sufficiently distinctive word to describe the aborigines of Australia to the exclusion of all other people — even if one uses a capital 'A'. Normally, in English, a plural noun is achieved by putting 's' on the end of the singular noun. This is not possible if 'aborigine' is to be avoided on Fowler's authority. To use Aboriginal and Aboriginals is consistent. To use Aboriginal also as adjective is to conform with the practice in use for people of other nationalities. Thus: I am German. I drive a German car. My parents are German. My parents are Germans.

Aboriginals themselves will eventually adopt words from a chosen Aboriginal language to describe all the members of their own racial group. This will probably happen when a particular language is selected by all Aboriginals as the lingua franca known as 'the Aboriginal language'. The nouns and adjectives chosen will then be adopted by the world on an official level, and hopefully that language will be taught in all Australian schools to all Australian children.

In the short term none of the words used on a regional basis to describe Aboriginals as a distinct group are known or understood or accepted by all Aboriginal people. Some (and to quote only a few of the better-known) words are:

Anangu, Tunuwuwi, Yolngu	(Northern Territory)
Murri	(Queensland)
Koori	(N.S.W., Victoria, Tasmania)
Nunga	(South Australia)
Nyunga, Marngu, Wonggai	(Western Australia)

In fact, some nouns used are either confusing or offensive to other traditional speakers. For example, 'murri' (mari) means 'trouble' in Arnhem Land languages; and 'nunga' means 'Chinese' in some Northern Territory languages and 'friend' in others.

To date, there is no lingua franca. Two languages, Pitjantjatjara from Central Australia and Gupapuyngu from Arnhem Land have been thoroughly researched and probably have more speakers, Aboriginal and non-Aboriginal, than the others. Because so many Aboriginal people in southern and eastern Australia have lost their own languages it is likely that one of those two languages will be adopted nationally.

It is estimated that in 1787 there were several hundred separate and distinct languages spoken in Australia. Two hundred years later, somewhat amazingly (given that Aboriginals have had such traumatic experiences), there are still over fifty languages in use as 'mother tongue' or 'first language' by around fifty thousand Aboriginals. Hopefully these languages will all be retained and consolidated even after a lingua franca called 'Australian' is recognised at international level.

Djaylama, a renowned dancer and spearthrower from Arnhem Land

Who Is This Book About?

This book and the songs on the companion L.P. record are about the Australian Aboriginals, past and present, but particularly those who have lived within the last two hundred years.

It is specifically not about the Torres Strait Islanders, who are a completely different racial group living within arbitrarily defined boundaries which also happen to declare them to be Australians. While the original Melanesian Torres Strait Islanders would also classify to be called 'aborigines' in respect of their own islands they are not the group of aborigines now called the Aboriginals. Torres Strait Islanders have on occasions combined with the Aboriginals for political reasons, but their culture and background are quite different from the Aboriginals. As such they deserve to be treated as a separate, identifiable group.

While the words 'black' and 'blacks' are now sometimes in use as noun singular and noun plural to describe any people with skin colouring ranging from light brown to jet black, this book does not seek to cover people other than Aboriginals who might refer to themselves as 'blacks'. There are some 'blacks' who for opportunistic or other reasons avail themselves of positive campaigns aimed at improving the lifestyle of Aboriginals, or who present themselves as being as underprivileged as Aboriginals. They tend to speak on behalf of Australia's 'blacks' without ever using the word 'Aboriginal'. This is a minor and understandable form of deception, but one of the problems for Aboriginals is that 'blacks' who have come from other countries are often pandered to and used to evoke unfavourable comment about Aboriginals. 'Why can't they be like Viv Richards?' is a rhetorical question sometimes asked.

Officially an Aboriginal is 'a person of Aboriginal descent who identifies as an Aboriginal and is accepted as such by other Aboriginals'. Thus the definition covers university graduates with pale skin and freckles, it includes people with blue eyes, and it includes people living in Arnhem Land and the Central Desert who possess the local knowledge, skills, language and ceremonies of their ancestors. Applying the age-old tactic of 'divide and rule' there are rantings from some reactionaries about 'yeller fellers on the bandwagon', and ravings about how 'I got on real well with the old style blackfeller but I can't stand these half-castes who have to invite discrimination'. What the reactionaries conveniently choose to overlook is that people of mixed Aboriginal descent have until recently been subjected to all kinds of hair-splitting, South African style counting of drops of blood in order that they may be discriminated against legally and effectively. Emotive, sometimes ridiculous and always offensive terms like 'fullblood' (who isn't full of blood?) 'part-coloured' (which part? what colour?) 'half-caste' 'quarter-caste' 'three-quarter caste' and 'octoroon' were the basis of legislation which determined, until the 1950s, that 'the Aboriginal part' of a person was the thing which *de facto* or *de jure* ordained that discrimination would be a permanent feature of that person's life.

Then, between the 1950s, and 1970s, within the framework of the government's 'assimilation' policy, mixed race people were bribed to deny their Aboriginality, being offered 'citizens rights' in order that they might become 'like whites'. Now, when Aboriginality is proclaimed on the basis of self-identification it is not simply allowed to be called pride in one's heritage. No, the reactionaries tell us, they're only 'getting on the bandwagon', looking for land, scholarships, housing loans and other things 'which we whites can't get'.

We are sometimes told that all residents of this country should be proud to be called, simply 'Australians'. So Aboriginals who for two hundred years have been discriminated against on the mere ground of their Aboriginality — which is physically obvious — are now accused of something almost sinister if they display pride in that same Aboriginality and in the fact that they are members of a race which lived in a harmonious, conservationist environment on this continent for at least forty thousand years before the place was called Australia.

In the 1980s a considerable amount of anti-Aboriginal literature was distributed, mainly by publishers with League of Rights and South African connections. The general aim was to discredit the Aboriginal land rights movement, mainly on the grounds that those in the forefront were 'part-whites' from city backgrounds who were only interested in political unrest and getting something for nothing. Another and even more sinister aim of these publications was to convince white Australians that, really, blacks were an ungrateful bunch who should not be given any leeway by superior whites. The obvious follow-on would be for the convinced, informed whites to take a pro-white stance in respect of South Africa, on the basis that 'we beleaguered whites must stick together'. One book, *Land Rights, Birth Rights,* noteworthy only for the incredible number of errors, typographical, orthographical and historical in its pages, purported to take the part of 'real' Aboriginals while putting down the 'part-whites' who were the cause of Australia's problems and unrest.

The specific case of the formal recognition of Aboriginal ownership of Uluru (Ayers Rock) was discussed in the book in terms which incorrectly inferred that ownership had been given, to the exclusion of all other 'Australians', to the Mutitjula community, many of whose 'part-white' members did not have real or traditional affiliations with 'The Rock'. The truth is that ownership of Uluru is vested in a Trust on behalf of *all* Aboriginals, deliberately unnamed, deliberately undefined, with a vested, traditional interest.

Again, in the book, it was alleged that the 'part-whites' are despised by the 'real Aboriginals' and that they should seek to be identified simply as 'Australians' by all other good Australians. It would be interesting to see the author, by extension of his arguments, telling the Welsh that they should call themselves English, or that Muhammud Ali, Vivian Richards and Dame Kiri Te Kanawa, being 'part-whites', have no right to flaunt any 'ethnic' background as they stride the world's stage.

Where Did All Those People Go?

It is estimated that in 1788 there were around 300,000 Aboriginals in Australia, including the island Tasmania. Two hundred years later the Aboriginal population is around 150,000, representing 1 per cent of the total population of Australia. Around 50,000 Aboriginals are of the full descent, and the total number represents those who themselves identify as Aboriginals on the census.

Captains Cook and Phillip were given official instructions to be kindly disposed towards any indigenous inhabitants they might encounter on this continent, and each was suitably solicitous on first contact. Governor Phillip went to great trouble to try to make useful contact with Aboriginals around Port Jackson. He was suitably impressed by their stature and demeanour and, indeed, named Manly Cove on the basis of the 'manly group' of Aboriginals he met there. The goodwill did not filter down to his troops and the convicts and very quickly there were problems. The Aboriginals were encouraged to come into the new settlement, but, when they arrived empty-handed and began to hang around, the whites were quick to chase them away. When it became obvious that the whites were not going to leave, and began to shoot kangaroos and fence off water supplies, the Aboriginals began to retaliate in different ways. It was not long before the disastrous effects of 'civilisation' on the Aboriginals began to be evident. The Europeans took some pleasure in supplying rum to Aboriginals, many of whom became hopeless drunkards, prepared to dance, fight, do anything for the temporary euphoria derived from the fiery spirit. Cook's 'noble savage' had become an object of scorn and ridicule in the settled areas, and a hated incendiarist and murderer on the spreading frontier. By the time Lachlan Macquarie arrived as Governor in 1810 it was felt that the Aboriginal 'problem' might best be resolved by the establishment of an institution for the adults and a school for the children.

When the Blue Mountains were crossed in 1813 settlement raced ahead of the law enforcement agencies, and frontier law prevailed. It may truly be said that this situation has never really been corrected in Australia: by the time the government arrives the *modus operandi* has been established and the government then legalises it. Such a situation has spelt absolute disaster for the Aboriginal race, whose moral and legal rights to their land have at all times been totally ignored or brutally suppressed. It took only forty years in Tasmania for the entire race of Aboriginals of the full descent to be eliminated — and this was forever. Forty years to annihilate a people, a language and a culture which had existed in absolute compatability with nature for forty thousand years, wiped out by drop-outs, convicts and thugs from a supposed civilisation twelve thousand miles away.

It is true that many things other than bullets contributed to the rapid decline of the Aboriginal population. Many thousands must have succumbed to the ongoing problems of wearing clothing which they had previously not needed. Diseases to which they had no immunity ravaged many tribes. In a male dominated group of newcomers it was inevitable that many men would seek sexual gratification from Aboriginal women. This in turn caused fights, and introduced venereal diseases and all the nefarious practices that go hand-in-hand with prostitution, principally payment with cheap and lethal alcohol.

All the above factors would have created problems for officials, and the usual 'solution' was to institutionalise the Aboriginal people. This simply compounded the problems in that it herded Aboriginals together with no regard for traditional conventions. It introduced them to inferior foodstuffs such as white flour and sugar, it upset the fine balance they had established with nature in their hunting and gathering lifestyle, and it inaugurated the standard corruptions of institutions which are as old as institutions themselves. Health standards deteriorated appallingly. Language began to disappear, and the failure to perform ceremonies would have further attenuated the important but fragile links with nature. Wild opinions about intrinsic flaws in the Aboriginal make-up began to be promulgated.

'Only in the cold winters of southern Australia did Aboriginals need to wear animal skin cloaks' (Photo Department of Aboriginal Affairs)

Because they had always been considered to be non-persons with no culture by the whites, their traditional lifestyle would at best have been ridiculed, but more likely in establishing institutions there would have been bans on things like traditional language, on the grounds that the only possible hope for Aboriginals lay in their becoming 'civilised'. Because at all times Aboriginals were an aggravating reminder that the land had in fact been stolen, race-hatred behavioural patterns and attitudes were established among whites on a peer group basis. This has not only prevailed, but has increased. Much of this is embodied in racist jokes and doggerel, often with a sexual theme, useful to allow those who had caused the depravity to demonstrate that they were capable of the most hate. Songs like the one about the 'Warrego gin with a bone through her nose and teeth like a Moreton Bay shark' would have been sung enthusiastically by the sires of the many thousands of children of mixed race born to Aboriginal women but not acknowledged by their white fathers.

A degraded, demoralised people often lose the desire to survive, and this must have applied to many Aboriginal groups who have disappeared completely. So the population was not merely being eliminated, there was for many years no regenerative factor either. It is estimated that by around 1900 the Aboriginal population was down to around 80,000.

The above reasons for population decline are tragic enough, but it must not be forgotten that the bullet wiped out countless thousands of Aboriginals, often in campaigns which can only be described as calculated murder. All sorts of euphemisms have been applied, like 'punitive expeditions' and 'retaliatory reprisals' and 'teaching the blacks a lesson' but in the vast majority of cases Aboriginals were murdered because they stood in the way of the easy annexation of their land. And often the massacres were carried out not just with tacit police approval, but with police riding in the forefront and with the support of their political masters. It is an indictment of Australia that there are still alive police and others who boast that they have shot unarmed Aboriginals. They should of course be charged with murder, but regrettably they attract many sycophantic listeners who 'yearn for the good old days'.

The ultimate treachery was in the use of Aboriginals from one area to assist in the shooting of another tribe, perhaps one with whom there was a traditional antipathy. In Queensland especially, the Native Police under their white commanders opened up thousands of square miles of country for white settlers in this manner. At the same time the Native Police underwrote their own extinction.

Professor Henry Reynolds, in a revealing book *The Other Side of the Frontier* (Penguin), points out that in many areas Aboriginals put up stubborn, organised and effective resistance, but he is nonetheless forced to the conclusion that in the 70 years between the first settlement in north Queensland and the 1930s as many as 10,000 Aboriginals were killed in encounters with Europeans in northern Australia. He compares this figure with the 5000 Europeans from north of the Tropic of Capricorn who died in the five international wars from the Boer War to Vietnam, a similar period of years. He then goes on (pp 200–1) to ask:

> How, then, do we deal with the Aboriginal dead? White Australians frequently say 'all that' should be forgotten. But it will not be. It cannot be. Black memories are too deeply, too recently scarred. And forgetfulness is a strange prescription coming from a community which has revered the fallen warrior, and emblazoned the phrase 'Lest We Forget' on monuments throughout the land…If we are to continue to celebrate the sacrifice of men and women who died for their country can we deny admission to fallen tribesmen?…If they did not die for Australia as such they fell defending their homelands, their sacred sites, their way of life.

There are still Aboriginal survivors of the last two massacres of Aboriginals, which were at Coniston, Northern Territory, in 1928, and Forrest River in the Kimberley region of Western Australia in 1931. At Coniston an official 31 men, women and children were shot by police and helpers, but a local clergyman who did a head-count based on known family groups put the number at certainly 80 and possibly one hundred. A Committee of Enquiry was convened — by the police — and surprise, surprise, the police were exonerated:

> '…the Board found the shooting was justified and that the natives killed in the various encounters were all members of the Walmulla tribe from Western Australia who were on a marauding expedition with the avowed objective of wiping out the white settlers and native boys employed on these stations'.

At Forrest River the massacre of twenty-eight men, women and children was carried out by a police constable who swore in two Aboriginals as 'trackers' to assist him and the pastoralists he engaged as 'special constables'. When the shooting was accomplished the party of whites took the two police trackers to the rubbish dump at Wyndham and shot them dead to prevent any prospect of dangerous evidence.

The world finally caught up with the Australian frontier. In 1933, following the justifiable killings of five Japanese trepangers, and two beachcombers who had stolen Aboriginal women, a police party was sent to eastern Arnhem Land. One policeman was killed by a spear and another had a spear through his hat. The police quickly withdrew, and plans were formulated the following year for a standard 'punitive expedition'. The police denied that this was their plan (although I hold the consignment note which accompanied the delivery to Darwin of rifles, shotguns, pistols, ammunition and binoculars) but it was public opinion, expressed at protest meetings attended by thousands of Australians in Melbourne and Sydney, which eventually caused the cancellation of the police plan.

It is appalling to record that many other Aboriginals were murdered deliberately through the issue of poisoned flour cooked into dampers, or through gifts of strychnine-laced 'pink sugar'.

It is not suggested that white people of today should wear sackcloth and ashes and prostrate themselves at the feet of Aboriginals. What is suggested is that our children should be taught historical facts in school, and that there should be skilfully designed educational programs to seek to reverse the situation whereby we learn to despise Aboriginals and to loathe things Aboriginal as a matter of course. A positive teaching program might even circulate among Australian children a resentment that, because of the brutality of the British colonial system, the greed with which the frontier was stolen and developed, and the consequent and ongoing denigration of Aboriginals, Australians generally have been denied the means to develop pride in the unique lifestyle and occupancy of this continent by Aboriginals.

At the moment, objective assessment of the facts can only lead to the conclusion that Australia's track record in colonisation is one of the worst on record.

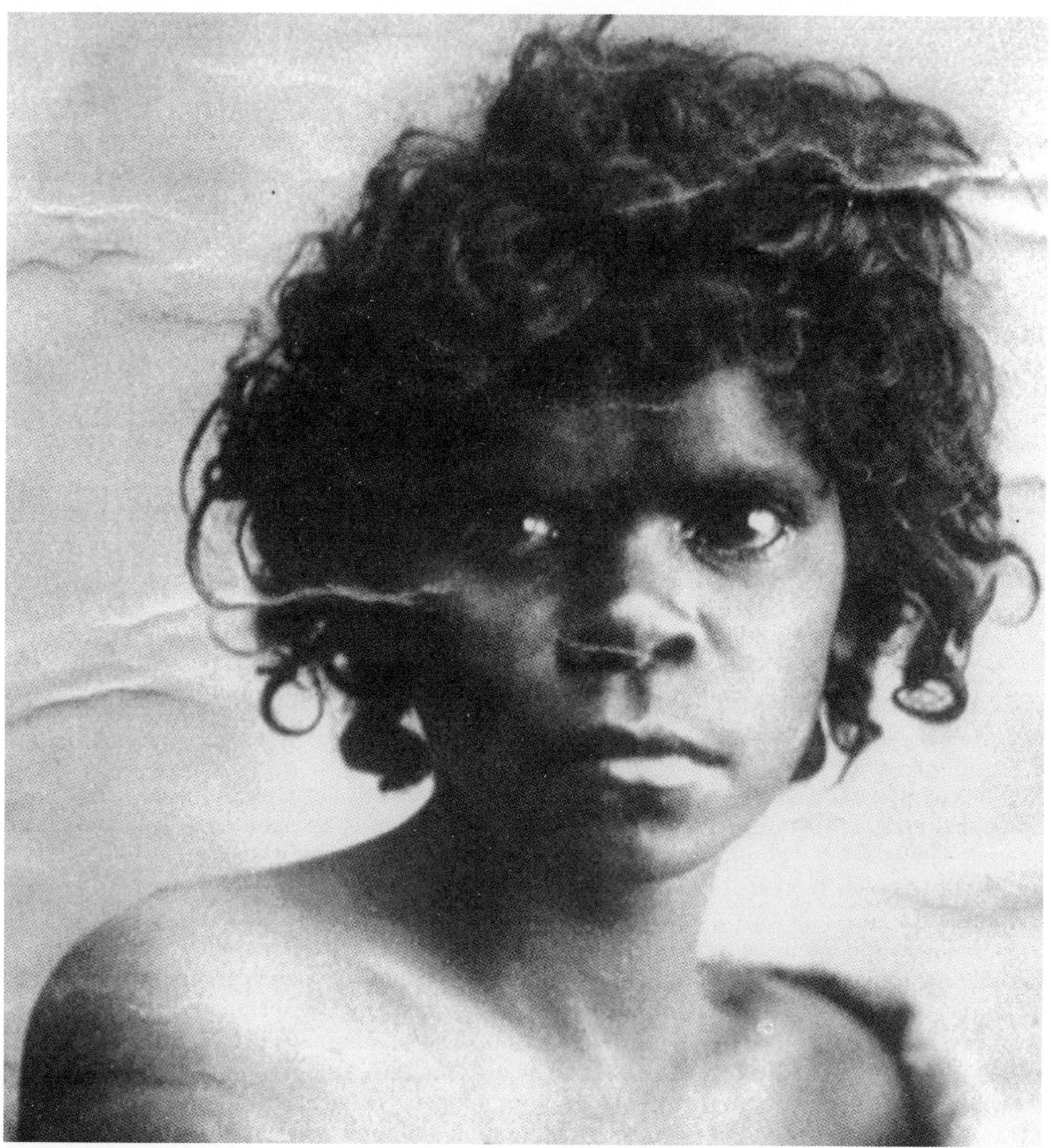

'In a male-dominated group of newcomers it was inevitable that many men would seek sexual gratification from Aboriginal women' (Photo Department of Aboriginal Affairs)

Traditional Aboriginal Lifestyle: A Brief Comment

Two factors are stressed as having great importance when considering Aboriginal traditions and customs still affecting the lives of many thousands of tribally oriented Aboriginals today.

Factor 1 The emphasis is on conservatism, and maintenance of the status quo. It would be interesting to know when the last significant change occurred, either in the form of a new invention, a new hunting technique, a new ceremonial adaptation, a change in marriage rules. In most areas it is probably safe to speculate that there would have been absolutely no change in the last ten thousand years. While most Aboriginals have been quick to compromise with the presence of non-Aboriginals, and wear clothes, drive motor cars, use money etc., their traditional life is kept quite separate. Most white people would be surprised to know just how strong and influential that lifestyle is. In many areas the ceremonial life has been strengthened because of various pressures to which Aboriginal groups have been subjected.

Factor 2 When a person is conceived, and right throughout life, a specific identity is allocated. That identity will pre-determine almost everything which happens in the person's life — who to love and respect, who to avoid, who to look after, who to fight with or against, who to marry and so on. And the complete detail of every person's identity must be known to all other people in order that behaviour may be modified and regulated accordingly.

Factor 1 will indicate just how difficult it is to effect change among Aboriginals, particularly if they resist that change. Factor 2 will indicate just how difficult it is for any Aboriginal to display individual initiative, for this is contrary to everything embodied in the traditional Aboriginal way of life.

Identity does not simply mean possession of a name. In the broadest terms it also means (a) membership of a tribe or language group (b) membership of a moiety (half) within the larger group, which begins to spell out things like who may marry whom (c) possession of a sub-section or 'skin' classification which further clarifies possible marriage partners (d) possession of a totemic affiliation which in turn determines a ceremonial role (e) membership of a clan which will determine an individual's right to land and food-collection (f) membership of an age/status group indicating seniority in initiation terms.

At some stage of a person's life — but not necessarily at birth — a personal name or names will be bestowed, and these names may or may not be used as public forms of address. It depends on location, but usually a personal name is very private and often goes out of use for a period of years, and sometimes forever, after a person's death. More often than not a person is addressed by a kinship term, a nickname, an initiation grade name or by a term indicating age or status. The comprehensiveness of these terms in Aboriginal languages is staggering. Among the Tiwi people of Bathurst and Melville Islands there are thirty precise kinship terms in common use, thirty-five age and status terms, and seven stages of initiation. As an example of this single-word comprehensiveness here are some of the terms:

timintinga	mother's brother's wife
ngentamilinga	sister's daughter's daughter
piniwini	wife's mother's brother
putaka	a woman bereaved of her brother or sister
ngunantani	a man bereaved of a child

When it is considered that every member of Tiwi society is required to learn, understand and use such terms, and to relate them to other factors like membership of twenty-one totemic groups and fourteen clans in order to establish and maintain proper behavioural patterns, assertions that Aboriginal society is either 'primitive' or 'simple' are shown to be nonsense.

Initiation

Because most of the early anthropological observations of Aboriginals were made by males the impression created was of a totally male-dominated society. It is now being recorded that women have an equally meaningful secret/sacred ceremonial life with similar restrictions on male participation or observation. And women, just as men, are entrusted with more and more 'inside' knowledge as their age, status and maturity determine. Unlike western society, children have no status, hence educational programs designed to effect societal change in children without reference to their parents are either doomed to failure or bound to create confusion and trouble.

There is more physical evidence of initiation ceremonies for males than females, and these ceremonies may include circumcision, sub-incision, tooth evulsion and cicatrisation. For women the concentration is on fertility song cycles with associated body painting, and songs relating to the hunting and gathering lifestyle. It is estimated that in a totally 'bush' existence women provide more than 80 per cent of the food, so a thorough indoctrination via ceremonies about tracking, locating, collecting, preparing, and, importantly, respecting the different food sources is vital. As a result, women are usually much better trackers than men, a fact which has generally eluded people such as police, who occasionally use Aboriginals as trackers.

Marriage

Intricate marriage laws have enabled Aboriginal people to live for thousands of years in small isolated communities and not become in-bred. Even if the rules are sometimes broken there are corrective means available to restore the balance. The following diagram gives a simplified idea of how the system works in one tribe, the Warlpiri (sometimes spelt Walbiri, Wailbri)

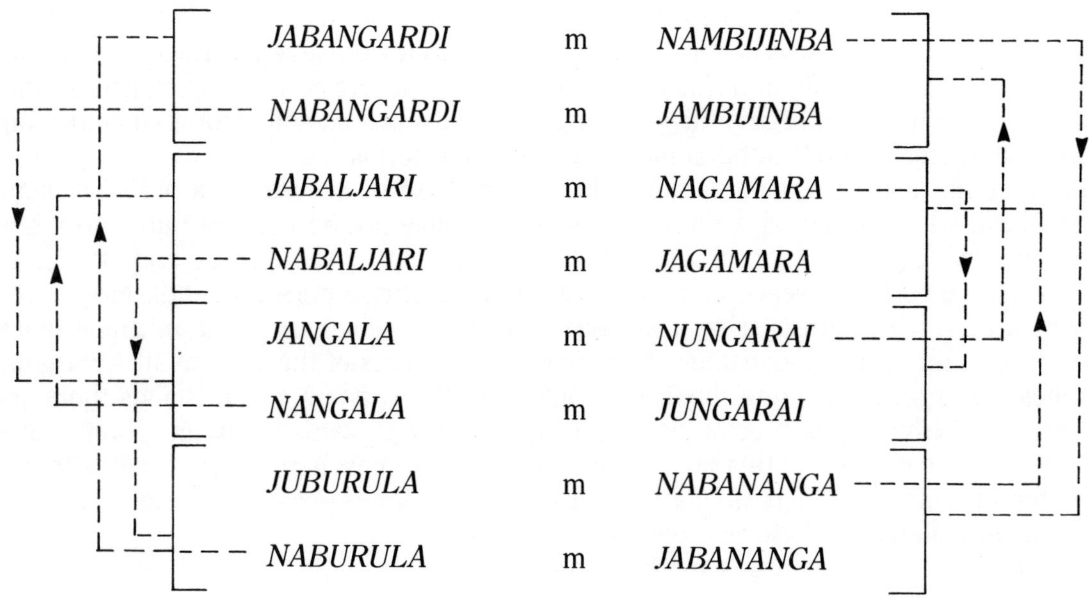

Every Warlpiri person is born into one of the eight (bracketted) groups above. In the bracketted pairs words beginning with 'j' are males, those beginning with 'n' are females. The linking 'm' shows (top line) that a 'jabangardi' man should marry a 'nambijinba' woman. Follow the arrow from the 'nambijinba' woman. Children from each marriage derive their identity (in anthropological terms, their 'sub-section') from the mother, so the sons from the marriage are 'jabananga' and the daughters are 'nabananga'. Trace the arrows from woman to woman to see how the pattern continues. There are complicated alternative marriages available. In straight genetic terms, mistakes or irregularities are corrected by the sub-section being derived from the mother and not the father or putative father.

Marriage in Aboriginal society was — and is — often polygamous, or, more correctly, polygynous. Marriages should be strictly organised and arranged, for there is little leeway for personal whim in a society which must avoid the possibility of in-breeding. There is a strong economic aspect to marriage, but it should not be thought that this precludes the normal range of emotional aspects as well.

Ceremonial Life

Increase rituals The main purpose of Aboriginal life is to live in complete harmony with nature. Importantly humans are not accorded superior status: the land and all its creatures, including humans, are one and inseparable. Any of the component parts in this total relationship is at risk if separated from its contact with the others.

The great ceremonies are organised to pay tribute to nature in all its forms: ceremonies for initiation, mourning or retribution are minor in significance. I witnessed most of a Kunapipi ceremony in Arnhem Land in 1957. Continuously for two months dances and songs were performed, regalia was exhibited and re-decorated, and in this way over two hundred adults ritualised their centuries-old, ongoing connection with the land, the sea, the universe and all its creatures. Thus they were assured of a benign relationship with their environment. Comparable ceremonies to ensure compatibility with nature are observed in most tribal regions.

Trade and Exchange The ceremonial exchange of trade goods and ceremonies is still a feature of Aboriginal society, although nowadays the exchange may be effected via aeroplanes rather than the long walks of earlier days. Ochres, weapons and ornaments, along with song cycles, have been traded among tribes for probably as long as Aboriginals have been on the continent. In Central Australia exchanges are still carried out by what is called the 'red ochre movement'. There are still alive today many men who have walked from the Great Australian Bight to Arnhem Land exchanging stage by stage song cycles and trade goods.

'Playabout' The degree to which Aboriginals engage in light-hearted singing and dancing, involving all members of the community, seems to vary according to the harshness of the environment and, by extension, the lifestyle. 'Playabout' corroborees are commonplace in Arnhem Land where food and water are plentiful, but unheard of in Central Australia where life was traditionally more arduous.

'Playabout' corroborees invariably are great fun, and the level of originality varies from group to group. This is the 'hearth', common to all races of the earth, where children learn the 'open' songs through constant repetition, where court jesters strut their stages, and where, occasionally, a very old person will suddenly find the energy to leap into the ring to show the young ones how it was done in the good old days. To people who have spent time in the far north of Australia there is nothing as reassuring as the drone of the didgeridoo, the clicking of sticks, and the sounds of uninhibited singing and dancing.

Fights, Duels and Peacemaking It smacks too much of 'noble savage' romanticism to suggest that fighting and duelling among Aboriginals are always ritualised and formalised, for there are often explosive displays of rage and violence which refute any ideas of prescribed rules

Ceremonial life is still strong in many parts of Australia. The Tiwi tribe of northern Australia (Photos by Allan Howard)

and conventions. Institutionalism and towns do not help, for they tend to throw together Aboriginals who should avoid one another. Alcohol is a tremendous problem, for its abuse tends to impair people's brains to the point where important rules and conventions are forgotten, passions are inflamed, and inbuilt inhibitions are cast aside.

Disputes do take place, and it is essential in small communities that these be resolved in starkly symbolic ways, rather than in total war which would decimate the population. There are two systems of ritualised fighting and peacemaking still capable of being implemented, provided land is unalienated and outsiders keep out of things. One is the 'Karintjukara' system of knife-duelling in Central Australia, where seconds are appointed to ensure that combatants only cut one another's backs to the point where honour is satisfied. Again, modern factors (and sometimes, alcohol) tend to militate against this system, in that steel knives are often used instead of the traditional stone knives, with disastrous results.

Another is the 'makarrata' peace-making ceremony from Arnhem Land. 'Makarr' (pronounced muck-are) means 'thigh' and 'makarrata' (pronounced muck -ARE-ra-ta, with the emphasis on the 'are') literally means 'one in the thigh', the name deriving from the trial-by-ordeal implemented to resolve grievances and restore peace. Traditionally in Arnhem Land grievances must be settled before other ceremonies can be held. Offenders have the complaints against them enunciated in no uncertain terms — and with suitable invective — by the aggrieved persons, their supporters and relations. The offender is required to stand in the open and have spears thrown at him (I have no knowledge of the makarrata applying to women). Because the main game played by young Aboriginal boys traditionally was spear-dodging, it should be relatively easy to dodge the spears effectively. But justice must be

Makarrata peace-making ceremony. This Anindilyaugwa (Groote Eylandt) man dances so that his crocodile totem will protect him when the spears are thrown. Women and children watch with casual interest (Photo by Fred Gray)

seen to be done, and eventually one of the aggrieved dances towards the offender, who presents his thigh for ritual spearing. Blood is spilt: honour is restored.

In the early 1980s a political movement, 'Makarrata', sought to have a treaty or compact drawn up between Aboriginals and the Federal Government in Australia, and to provide for future situations where Aboriginal rights would be devolved, acknowledged and legally established. The term 'makarrata' was used synonymously for 'treaty'. The movement withered on the vine of political reality. It became obvious on the one hand that public opinion was hardening against Aboriginals; and on the other hand Aboriginal activists saw the movement as yet another attempt by do-gooding whites to impose their ideas on Aboriginals.

Death, Mourning and the Afterlife

The level of concern about a person's death is usually determined by the age or initiation status of the deceased. In the case of a young child the death will not unduly affect those outside the immediate family mourners, whereas the death of a respected old person will involve all. The unanticipated death of an able bodied person from sudden sickness, accident or other abnormal cause is likely to cause upheaval as people look for a reason and a culprit.

In older days bodies were disposed of by burial, or by exposure to the elements on rock shelves, in caves, or on tree platforms. In some areas a buried body is (even today) disinterred after a period, the skeleton carefully re-assembled, the bones cleaned, painted, and then lodged inside a hollow log coffin. The log coffin is then itself buried, usually after being carried around the region for ceremonies. After the final disposal of the bones or body a mourning ceremony is usually held.

Mourning The aim of mourning ceremonies is to appease the spirit of the deceased, to pay tribute, and to express sorrow in realistic, ritual and purgative terms. The immediate death of a person might prompt self-inflicted 'sorry' cuts or burns; and in Central Australia the thighs of most adult Aboriginals bear huge scars incurred thus. The forehead bleeds profusely and obviously, and it is common to wield a sharp stick or stone to self-inflict wounds to the forehead, while wailing and keening announce the death to all others.

The arranged mourning ceremonies, which usually take place months after death are quite often boisterous, busy and joyful. The deceased's clothing and belongings may be ceremonially burned, and then songs and dances are performed in order that the spirit of the deceased might quite happily return to its totemic origins. An important aspect of such ceremonies is the need to appease the deceased's spirit so it will not return to cause mischief among the living.

Probably the most unique mourning ceremony is the 'Pukamani' conducted by the Tiwi several months after a person's death. Huge and intricately carved poles (tudinni) are erected around the grave, the number and size of these being determined by the age and status of the deceased. Bark baskets are placed on top of the poles, and men, women and children participate in the ceremonies. Faces and bodies are painstakingly painted in elaborate, totemic patterns. Joyful, frenzied dancing and singing marks the end of the period of mourning, and the end of various prohibitions incurred by relatives during that period. The Tiwi are happy people, and this is a typical Tiwi farewell.

The Tiwi conduct elaborate Pukumani (mourning) ceremonies for the dead. Depending on the status of the deceased, grave posts called tudinni are erected and mourners perform their individual totemic dances. Melville Island, 1911 (Photo Department of Aboriginal Affairs)

Terra Nullius: Land Belonging to No One

'All land in Australia is held in consequence of an assumption so large, grand and remote from actuality that it had best be called royal, which is exactly what it was.'

W E H Stanner *After the Dreaming* (Boyer Lectures 1968)

There are many fine, and some definitive books, about Aboriginals written from historical and anthropological perspectives (see Bibliography). In the hope that this songbook, and the companion L.P. record will take the form of provocative entertainment, some background to the Aboriginal people's occupancy of this continent is provided here. I will often use the past tense but I deplore the exclusive use of that tense in writings about Aboriginals. Although many have been dispossessed and have no contact with the traditional lifestyle, there are nonetheless around fifty thousand Aboriginals who still speak their traditional languages and possess the skills and knowledge to enable them to live off the land. They still conduct ceremonies and observe laws which would have prevailed in 1787.

On 25 January 1788, the day before Captain Phillip landed at Sydney Cove with the First Fleet, the whole of Australia was occupied by the Aboriginals. It was divided among groups in a manner understood and respected by all. During the first two hundred years of white settlement the newcomers and their descendants have gradually taken over most of the fertile parts of Australia. In doing so they showed scant, if any, regard for any Aboriginal rights, legal or moral, in that land.

So in considering the history of Australia everything must be viewed against the fact that the land was originally stolen from the Aboriginals. The British merely legalised the theft.

The British Constitution empowers the Crown to exercise sovereign rights within its dominions. During the periods of colonial expansion it was assumed that sovereignty could be established in several different ways. One mode of acquisition lay in the application of the *terra nullius* doctrine where the land in question 'belonged to no one' or was 'not under the sovereignty of any state'.

Though strictly referring to uninhabited land the *terra nullius* doctrine was also extended by the British to cover the acquisition of any territory occupied by people whose level of civilisation was considered to be less developed than, and whose political organisation did not correspond to, European norms.

Thus with classical British impunity Captain Cook and later Captain Phillip laid claim to parts of the Australian continent. Claims were extended at colonies such as Swan River until the entire mainland of Australia plus the island of Tasmania had been annexed. The land holding authority was gradually devolved to the separate colony/states, and in 1901 the six states federated to become the Commonwealth of Australia.

Until 1970 there was no challenge to the British system of government, nor to the laws which legitimised the original thefts. In physical terms the occupancy was not as straight-forward as many have been led to believe, for in many frontier areas Aboriginals resisted the newcomers quite effectively. But eventually the gun conquered the spear.

It must be remembered that even today many Aboriginals see no need for legal challenge. Those retaining language, law and custom assume at all times that they have inviolable sovereignty over their land going back to time immemorial. Their security in their Aboriginality is at the same time their greatest strength and their absolute vulnerability.

In settled areas there were sporadic claims by Aboriginals that 'this is our land' but the powerful and numerically strong new settlers treated such claims with at best disdain but mainly ridicule.

In 1970 in the Supreme Court of the Northern Territory, in the case *Milirrpum v Nabalco and the Commonwealth of Australia* a group of Aboriginal clan leaders from Yirrkala, Arnhem Land, challenged the authority of the Commonwealth to lease land to Nabalco, a mining company. The Aboriginals lost the case, and there were considered to be no satisfactory grounds for appeal. In his judgement Justice Blackburn sympathised with the Aboriginal claimants, but held that they had not established their present relationships with the land as being the same as their ancestors in 1788. Justice Blackburn applied a principle of law known as *inter-temporal* law. According to this principle an assessment of the legal validity of a claim to land title or sovereignty is to be appreciated in the light of the law prevailing at the time of the original claim, and not in terms of the law in force at the time when a dispute regarding the original claim arises.

So in British legal terms Britain certainly did acquire sovereignty over Australia, a sovereignty which no other nation has ever challenged.

The above notwithstanding it was agreed by most political leaders that if Australia was to be given credibility in sensitive international issues there was a moral obligation to provide some sort of justice to Aboriginals in terms of 'land rights'.

The power of the Commonwealth to legislate in respect of Aboriginals lay in Section 51 (xxvi) of the Constitution which has been amended by a Holt Government inspired referendum in 1967. It now read that the Commonwealth had power 'to make laws in respect of the people of any race for whom it is deemed necessary to make special laws'. In Australia it is extremely difficult to achieve Constitutional change by referendum, for a referendum must be passed by a majority of electors in a majority of states and given an overall numerical majority. Many people have pointed with satisfaction to the fact that this particular referendum, empowering the Federal Government to legislate for Aboriginals, was passed with an 87 per cent 'yes' vote. What is more and ominously significant in my opinion is that there was a 13 per cent 'no' vote in what was basically a referendum to classify Aboriginals as human beings. For the referendum was also about things like the right to vote, and the right to be counted as 'people' at census times, and the right to be not discriminated against on grounds of race. Predictably the 'no' votes came largely from areas where there was a significant Aboriginal presence, where ethnocentrist and anti-Aboriginal attitudes prevailed and where racist standards were the norm.

The Aboriginal Land Rights Commission was set up by the Whitlam Government, and the Royal Commissioner was Justice A E Woodward. Woodward had appeared for the Aboriginals in the Yirrkala case, and like all counsel and the judge in that case he had acquired a considerable knowledge of anthropology. Under the terms of the Royal Commission Woodward was instructed not to establish **whether** Aboriginals could be given title to land but **how** this was to be achieved.

Powers over land still lay constitutionally with the States, and it was quickly apparent that the Commonwealth would be a toothless tiger in respect of Aboriginal land rights in the six states. The Fraser Government passed the Northern Territory *Land Rights Act*, for in the Northern Territory the Commonwealth's control was paramount. Under the terms of this Act all Aboriginal Reserves were handed over to land councils which were also set up under the Act. Several land inquiries were held, some pastoral properties were purchased on behalf of Aboriginals and speedily and effectively 25 per cent of the land of the Northern Territory was under Aboriginal ownership and title. The reasonable fact that 25 per cent of the N.T. population was now in control of 25 per cent of the land — usually land deemed to be useless for white settlement — did not prevent politicians in the conservative N.T. Government from whipping up hysteria constantly to remind voters that a *bête noire* named Whitlam had sold them out. The N.T. Government, given inordinate support from a highly politicised public service, has constantly pressed for power over land rights to be vested in itself. The Commonwealth has at all times resisted this in the knowledge that the Northern Territory had to be the yardstick for providing national land rights justice for Aboriginals but the performance of the Federal Government has been disappointing in national terms.

The Hawke Government proclaimed rather lamely that 'uniform land rights' was its policy. Probably with great relief this was shelved when in the 1985 West Australian state election Premier Burke said that his State had no intention of allowing any Commonwealth legislation in the field of land rights. This slap on the wrist from a fellow Labor politician came when Burke had done the political sums after a successful but incredibly biased and racist television campaign had been implemented by mining interests and backed up by Neanderthal rubbish purporting to be anthropologically based opinions from mining leaders. We may rest assured that in Australia no political party will ever again espouse 'uniform land rights' as its policy. And that may be for the best, given the differences prevailing among Aboriginal people. Tasmania and the Northern Territory are poles apart both geographically and Aboriginally. Traditional Aboriginal land affiliations can, and must be recognised in the Northern Territory: sadly, the same affiliations in Tasmania, based on ongoing performances of ceremonies with the consequent spiritual beliefs and practices, are gone for ever.

Justice in land is possible, and necessary for every Aboriginal person in Australia. Policies must in every case be arbitrary, but in the knowledge that a 'uniform' policy will not get to first legislative base the challenge is for courageous political and administrative action which will quickly and effectively come to terms with the problem. If Australia does not wish to continue to be classified with South Africa as an international pariah the leaders of this country must quickly pick up the Aboriginal land rights ball, which is very definitely in their court. It will also be important for politicians to say what they will *not* do, for white landholders very definitely have rights too. A courageous, honest promotional campaign must accompany a sound Aboriginal land policy to try to regain the ground where 87 per cent of white Australians might again be favourably disposed towards Aboriginals achieving justice. The mining leaders and the reactionary politicians in our midst have been very effective in their campaigns to denigrate Aboriginals: the challenge is for those with a social conscience, an understanding of the history of the country and an international rather than a parochial, short-term perspective, to desentimentalise and depoliticise Aboriginal issues promptly. Land justice for every Aboriginal group in Australia is a necessary first step.

White Man

Words and Music: Peter Knight
(Steeleye Span)

Chords repeat **12/8**   C – G F | C – G F ‖ **all the way.**

Moderate Tempo

know who they were, they were the ones whose sons and daugh-ters are do-ing it still. (We)
And in their hearts what did they feel? Did they
think they had the right to steal an - o-ther man's
land that had no name. O they
Fine
did - n't think he'd feel the pain, So
they sailed a - way from their own coun - try to an - o - ther man's land far a -
cross the sea, And they stole that land from the peo - ple there, And they
called that land Aus - tra - li - a. Why did he do it White
man? Why did he do it White man? Why did he do it White
1.
man? Why did he do it?
2.
man? Why did he do it? And in their
D.S. al Fine

Some sing of their glory
Few tell the true story
Most men they don't need it
White man he kills for it.

They took to the seas
Searching for a land that they could call Paradise
Stealing the breeze that carried them towards
     the Sun
With lust in their eyes and a gun in their hand
They said we've found Paradise
Think of the glory, look at the prize we've won.

We know who they were
They were the ones who killed their brothers
To steal from others
We know who they were
They were the ones whose sons and daughters
Are doing it still.

And in their hearts what did they feel?
Did they think they had the right to steal
Another man's land that had no name?
O they didn't think he'd feel the pain.

So they sailed away from their own country
To another man's land far across the sea
And they stole that land from the people there
And they called that land Australia.

Why did he do it
White man?

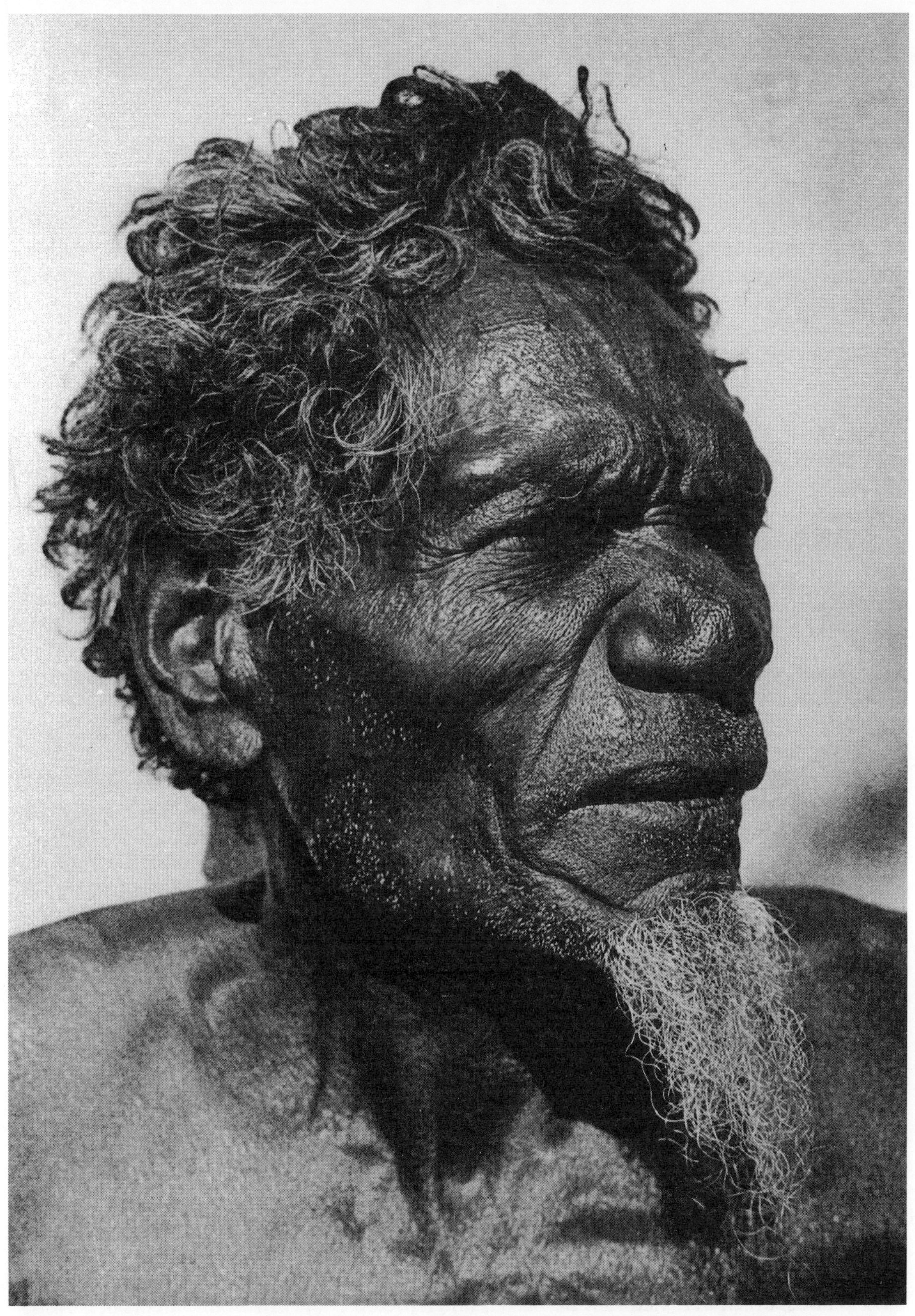

Mawalan Marika, the original Riratjingu plaintiff in the Yirrkala legal challenge. Mawalan was a famous painter on bark. Picasso once saw a Mawalan bark painting and said, 'Ah…if I could paint like that'

The First Political Victim: Benelong

The captures of Arabanoo, Colby and Benelong have often been written up as the means whereby Governor Phillip could demonstrate that he was 'favourably disposed towards the natives'. Watkin Tench, Surgeon to the first fleet, who has been called 'that liberal and candid mind', points out that there was probably a second and more important motive: prior to the arrival of the Second Fleet the settlement was close to starvation, so Phillip was anxious to find out what resources the country might have.

Arabanoo, the first man captured, died from smallpox, an ominous sign of things to come. It would be nice to know more about the resourceful Colby who 'slipped his hobbles' and escaped after a week. Benelong does not emerge as a giant of history, and probably does not deserve to. Because he is the first Aboriginal of whom the rest of the world has knowledge, and because he was the first person 'used' by the new system, to the point of dissipation and degradation, he is worthy of scrutiny.

With high minded propriety Benelong's captors described him variously as 'a bouncy, ebullient man', one who was 'tender with children', 'a bit of a comedian' and 'something of a rogue'. His opinion of his captors is not known.

It was estimated that he was around twenty-five years of age when captured in November 1789. He was hobbled, but allowed to walk around the settlement under supervision. After five months he escaped. No more was heard of him until September 1790 when he was recognised in a group of 200 Aboriginals, one of whom threw a spear which wounded the Governor. This was at the place which Phillip had previously called Manly Cove, after a meeting with a 'manly' group of Aboriginals.

Things were markedly different in 1791. The settlers had been reassured: they would not starve. To their annoyance Aboriginals now came in large, mendicant numbers, and many of them, Benelong included, became addicted to rum, the fiery currency of the time.

Phillip quite obviously had some affection for Benelong, for he had a hut built for him at what is now called Benelong Point, the site of the Sydney Opera House. There are reports that many settlers and convicts resented the favouritism shown to Benelong by the Governor.

In December 1792, at the end of Phillip's term as Governor, he took Benelong back to England with him. Again, it would be fascinating to know Benelong's reaction to the journey, and the pomp and circumstance of London, where he was dressed in the livery of the time and paraded as a 'noble savage' curiosity. Benelong's health deteriorated in the English climate, and he was understandably homesick. He would have been petrified at the thought of dying away from his 'dreaming'. In September 1795, before another cold English winter was to begin, Benelong was sent back to Australia on H.M.S. *Reliance*.

He died at Kissing Point on 3 January 1813, aged about fifty years. The *Sydney Gazette* of 9 January 1813 contained a scathing editorial:

> Bennelong (sic) died on Sunday morning last at Kissing Point. Of this veteran champion of the native tribe little favourable can be said. His voyage to, and benevolent treatment in Great Britain produced no change whatever in his manner and inclinations, which were naturally barbarous and ferocious. The principal Officers of Government had for many years endeavoured, by the kindest of usage, to wean him from his original habits, and draw him into a relish for civilised life; but every effort was in vain exerted, and for the last few years he has been but little noticed. His propensity

to drunkenness was inordinate; and when in that state he was insolent, menacing, and overbearing. In fact, he was a thorough savage, not to be warped from the form and character that nature gave him, by all the efforts that mankind could use.

What a pity he could not have written his memoirs. For apart from the patronising or derogatory things whites wrote or said about him we have no knowledge of Benelong the Aboriginal. Nobody learnt or recorded his language, nobody made any study of the Aboriginal people of Port Jackson. And there are none of them left. Not one.

When I spent a couple of reflective hours at the place now called Mrs Macquarie's Point, which I understand was called Yurong by Benelong's people, I felt robbed, deprived of the detail of that part of my country's history, which should have been recorded by somebody, somehow. By the time he got back from England Benelong must have been quite fluent in English and capable of the most unique observations.

As I thought about Benelong I speculated on the questions I would have asked him, and the things he might have told me. My experience with tribal men of similar age tells me that very early in our conversation he would have told me of his pukui, his 'spirit' or 'dreaming' or 'totem' if you like. The Tiwi equivalent is 'pukui' and every Tiwi person will quickly identify his or her 'pukui', for it is an integral part of a person.

Fancifully, as I watched a white sea eagle soar above the seagulls, above the white sails of the Opera House on Benelong Point I let my imagination run and began to write my song *The White Sea Eagle*. But it was pure speculation.

The White Sea Eagle

Words and Music: Ted Egan

Country Feel

36

CHORUS

As I stood by Mrs Macquarie's chair
In the knowledge that Benelong once
    stood there
A strange, chilling feeling came upon me
I seemed to hear a mournful song
The click of boomerangs as Benelong
Sang to his spirit, the white sea eagle

Ngananana ngaiyu ga nara muruganga
Ngananana ngaiyu ga nara muruganga
Ngananana ngaiyu ga nara muruganga
Ga nara muruganga ngaiyu ngananana.

There was an eerie sense of history on Yurong
It seemed haunted by the spirit of the man
    named Benelong
And I couldn't help thinking of that fateful day
The day that Governor Phillip came to stay
The day the white sea eagle flew away.

The eagle flew up into the sky
And it soared above the cliff-tops high
It screeched down its message to Benelong
'Beware', was the warning call
But the people ran off, one and all
To see the white man's ships as they rolled in.

I couldn't help thinking that Benelong
Never again sang the eagle song
For he seemed just like a man whose spirit
    left him
Doomed was he forever more
He lost his way as he lost his law
And the white sea eagle sings its song alone.

Genocide

We are told of holocausts, pogroms and the like. Although the scale may be smaller than Hitler's Germany or Stalin's Russia or Turkey's Armenia, Australia is the only country in the world where genocide has been completely achieved.

I defer to those people of mixed descent who justifiably lay claim to being Tasmanians in the truest sense of the term: may they achieve justice. But the cold, hard, inescapable fact is that it took the British only forty years to wipe out, for ever, every Tasmanian Aboriginal of the full descent.

I find it almost obscene that Truganini, or any other unwitting Tasmanian Aboriginal is put under academic scrutiny in respect of the extermination of their people. They never had a chance.

This pathetic photo shows Truganini (left) with three other Oyster Bay (Tas) Aboriginals of the full descent (Photo Department of Aboriginal Affairs)

Truganini

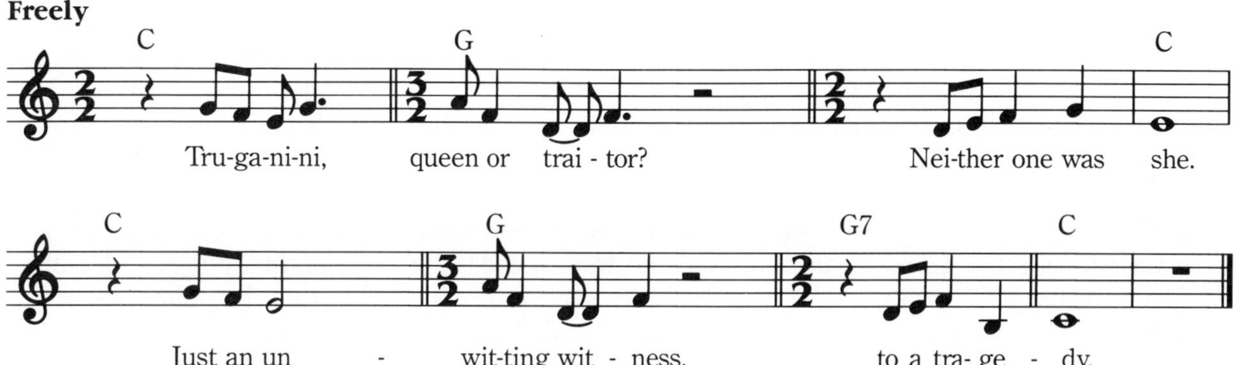

Truganini, queen or traitor?
Neither one was she
Just an unwitting witness
To a tragedy.

Forty years, start to finish
All her people gone
Banished she to the care of
George Robinson.

Never once did Truganini
Have a chance to say
What was best for her people
As they passed away.

When she died, Truganini,
Was put on display
No Dreamtime for her spirit
Exhibit 'A'.

Given back to her people
A hundred years had passed
Finally she was cremated
Rest in Peace at last.

Truganini, queen or traitor?
Neither one was she
Just an unwitting witness
To a tragedy.

The Massacres

The function of a uniform is to bestow on the wearer the trappings of authority. The uniform proclaims its wearer as an official ambassador of the power system it represents. The policy to be followed by the uniform wearers is usually clouded by euphemisms, legal mumbo-jumbo and vague clauses about things like 'sufficient force'. But the uniform wearers are usually confronted with real, rather than hypothetical situations, so they need to have an 'understanding' of what their masters will let them get away with, even if the masters are not necessarily going to condone what was done in their name, even if it does not seem to conform with the stated policy.

The large scale massacres of Aboriginals in Australia were all given tacit approval in this way. The perpetrators of the massacres almost invariably wore uniforms, and none were punished — which highlights again the difference between policy and practice. For not only was there no policy which said: 'We will exterminate all these people who stand in the way of our legal occupation of this land we call Australia' but, on the contrary, official policy was usually couched in language meant to show future historians that the policy makers were 'enlightened for the time' or 'surprisingly solicitous for the welfare of the natives'.

So around the 1988 bicentenary in Australia Governor Phillip is played by aspiring Oliviers in school pageants as a noble man, a man of stately bearing (you see, the uniform does that, even if the wearer never opens his mouth). He is represented as the man who seems determined to do what his masters in the Admirality seem to have instructed him to do. Phillip wants, in his own words 'to give the natives a high opinion of their new guests'. It is never stressed that Phillip would have known, when he demanded 'heads in bags' as he authorised the first punitive expedition in 1790, that he would get away with this sort of legalised murder. So, like Brutus, he is portrayed as an honourable man, but, unlike Brutus, not revealed in his true colours. For the final act has not been written.

Rarely did those at the top of the uniformed scale do the actual killing. Usually that was left to underlings, a Constable Murray, a Constable Regan, a Constable Wiltshire, sometimes even a Sub-Inspector Urquhart if the job was big enough, definitely a body of Native Police who invariably displayed 'primitive savagery' when killing their own. Thus if things really went wrong a scapegoat would not be hard to pinpoint. It was completely atypical for Governor Stirling himself to have taken part in the one-sided slaughter which historians seem intent on calling the 'battle' of Pinjarra. Some battle. Stirling must not only have been a very frustrated man, he must also have been fairly sure of his official standing.

The individual massacres have been detailed in the various books and I choose here not to list statistics, or to try to establish things like whether any of the various estimates of how many Kalkadoon were killed are true. I wish simply to point out that the major massacres were officially condoned. Sometimes they were organised in retaliation for other murders, but they were nonetheless official murder organised on a large scale by the community leaders who have streets and suburbs named after them.

It was once proposed in Darwin that a street be named Nemarluk Drive. A police inspector complained that streets 'should not be named after murderers'.

Teach the Blacks a Lesson

Words and Music: Ted Egan

Fast, driving rhythm

Aboriginal prisoners in chains, Wyndham, WA (Photo by Dame Mary Durack)

CHORUS

Teach the blacks a lesson was the message as
    they saddled up their horses
Teach the blacks a lesson was the cry as they
    handed out the guns
Are we not white? With a God-given right
To take this land and bend it to our will?
Do we not have legal power to kill?

When McIntyre was speared at Botany Bay
Captain Phillip sent his men away
'Bring me heads in bags' the Governor said,
'My personal huntsman McIntyre is dead'.
No matter what that hunting man had done
A most important point must be made
'We'll show these creatures once and forever
Authority is meant to be obeyed'.

Stirling said: 'I'm fed up with these Nyungahs
Yagan and his people have to go
We have to demonstrate that we are powerful
We'll show these blacks just what they need to
    know'.
So they rode in righteous splendour to Pinjarra
English gentry out to have some sport,
Quite a bit like hunting after foxes
Just another battle bravely fought.

When the squatters wanted dirt in western
    Queensland

They said: 'Clear it free of blacks and do it soon'.
So they sent the famous murderer Mr. Urquhart
With his Native Police to fight the Kalkadoon.
And so it came about on Battle Mountain
The spear was pitted up against the gun
Urquhart was promoted to Inspector
The Kalkadoons lay bleaching in the sun.

When Wiltshire shot the blacks up on the Daly
His masters were very, very keen
To know how many innocents he'd murdered
And how good had his Martini-Henry been.
He said: 'It's quite the perfect type of weapon,
Excellent for children on the run'.
So he wrote his book and modestly took credit
For the pioneering work he'd bravely done.

When old Fred Brooks was murdered out at
    Coniston
It didn't take too long to hear the call
Murray and his men rode out quickly,
'Don't apprehend the murderer: kill them all'.
So they signed up all the local whites as specials
'Men, women and children have to go'.
They shot the Walbiri down on the Lander
And officialdom recorded: *quid pro quo*.

The Soft Steal: Institutions

The title for my song *Bullocky's Joy and Jesus* came from my observation of the system in operation on a particular Aboriginal mission station. Aboriginals were expected to attend church each morning, and were given a metal token to prove attendance. Then, on ration day, if they presented seven tokens they were given the full ration of flour, tea, and sugar, plus a bonus tin of treacle. Treacle is called 'Cockie's Delight' or 'Bullocky's Joy' in the bush. Six tokens, no treacle. No tokens, no rations.

Nowadays it is hard to convince Aboriginals that the institutional process was not a calculated, sinister plot to entice them off their land in order that it might more easily be taken over by white settlers and, latterly, miners. Such is the wisdom of hindsight.

It is true that the very establishment of mission stations and government settlements did cause the vast majority of Aboriginals to leave their traditional country in order to enjoy the dubious benefits of the white man's lifestyle. Some were coerced, but the vast majority of Aboriginals voluntarily succumbed to the offers of flour, tea, sugar, treacle, tobacco, clothing and blankets. By the time they woke to the fact that the white man was fairly mean when it came to distributing these goodies most were entrapped, particularly by the fact that their children had been enrolled in schools.

In fairness to some fine people who staffed some mission stations in pioneering days it must be said that many of them were motivated by the highest ideals, and developed such affinity with Aboriginals that any suggestion that they might be undermining the very structure of Aboriginal society would have appalled them. These were not principals of missionary societies, but missionaries in the field; and nowhere near enough has been written to record the fine, selfless work undertaken in the face of incredible hardship. Many books have been published about missionaries, but these are mostly written by other missionaries and from an evangelical rather than a practical point of view — 'He laboured and the Lord smiled' — sort of thing, which highlights another problem: many people working among Aboriginals are really there for their own good, or looking for some reward in the next life, and not for the real benefit of the Aboriginals whose interests they purport to serve.

It must be stated too, especially in relation to frontier areas, that had not some mission societies exerted pressure to get leases in their own names over Aboriginal land the same land would long since have been lost to those Aboriginals who now own it freehold. It is not too melodramatic to say that in some areas there would be no Aboriginals left if it had not been for the protection, in the real sense of the term, of the missionaries. Among the better mission societies valuable research has been carried out, sound work has been done on recording languages and genealogies, and in educating Aboriginal people to carry on this task. Quite often health and general standards from 'point of contact' have been improved considerably by the presence of self-effacing workers who have toiled lifetimes and for little if any pay.

It is a fact, nonetheless, that even on the very best of mission stations and government institutions tremendous problems have been created for Aboriginal people in the future, simply because the lifestyle which has been imposed on Aboriginals is so different from that which prevailed traditionally. In traditional Aboriginal society the emphasis is on no change, and thereby decision-making is anathema. Things happen slowly and naturally, because everybody, and especially old people, knew (and know) the correct behavioural procedure for every situation. They also know the answers to every question which could conceivably arise in their society, because conventions have developed intrinsically over countless centuries. There is no hard and fast 'tribal law' but often today there are calls from Aboriginals to 'let us settle this matter the tribal way'. These pleas usually come from sophisticated Aboriginals, often far removed from the traditional lifestyle. Their claims to status often lie only in their ability to articulate in English. Very often the 'tribal solutions' they would impose are some barbaric extension of things they have observed in white society.

With the establishment of institutions for Aboriginals came the presence of the white officials, some good, some bad, some intelligent, some dumb, but all wanting a result either in physical or spiritual terms or both. The best result for a person working in an Aboriginal community for fifty years should be to say, 'Well, I got the best possible result, nothing whatsoever happened'. That would be totally unacceptable to a white society where people are only judged on results. So practical, workaholic whites have been only too happy to become the decision-makers in Aboriginal society. Oh, it's all wrapped up in the proper jargon. There must be 'consultation'. There must be local councils. The 'people' will be heard. They will have houses but only the type they really want. They will decide this, that, and the other.

It is too often forgotten that in traditional Aboriginal society there are so many in-built safeguards, one of these being an almost excessive politeness. In small communities lack of politeness can cause argument which causes conflict which becomes vendetta for the next hundred years. So when our enthusiastic official, who has spent hours, perhaps days, working something out, thinking it through and perhaps drawing plans and diagrams comes to 'the council of elders' for 'consultation' to announce the scheme as 'only ideas, mind' there is quick reassurance forthcoming via murmurings of approval and loud cries of 'yes boss'. So 'boss' (having reminded people that such titles are out and that only kinship terms or first names are acceptable as forms of address in the new scheme of things) goes off and does the job, perhaps thinking that the Aboriginals are either 'cute' or 'a lazy mob of

'Ring the bell. Go to School. Teach us all the Golden Rule'. The faces of the children tell us how much they are enjoying school on this mission station (Photo Department of Aboriginal Affairs)

so-and so's'. Or perhaps a word of prayer is offered as thanks for being able to work on such a you-beaut, consultative basis with 'my people'.

Given such positive opportunity for manipulating an entire race of people whose silence or polite response is taken to imply assent, the total institutionalisation process has largely been counter-productive. Administrator has followed administrator, each with a new set of policies perhaps diametrically opposed to those of the previous regime. An indication of the real effect this has had on Aboriginal people can be seen in some of the large government settlements established in the Northern Territory in the 1950s. As part of the 'assimilation' policy, whereby it was deemed that all Aboriginals should 'become like us' in one lovely unified Australian society, huge artificial towns were built, providing schools, hospitals, communal kitchens where everybody ate three cooked meals a day, cinemas and houses for all, with the standard of housing being dependent on the level of 'assimilability'. Now that 'self-determination' is the latest policy imposed on Aboriginals by a never-decreasing tribe of white advisors, those showplaces have been reduced to vandalised ruins and Aboriginals have elected to go back to much more basic but happier homelands. Surely this is an indication that we didn't get the message across, or that we were wide of the mark in assuming that Aboriginals would want to be like us. And sadly, Aboriginals get blamed into and out of every policy: they get blamed for not having developed the initiative to build towns, and then they get blamed for allowing their children to wreck the towns that were imposed on them.

If the end result on the better institutions has been the creation of tremendous problems, what can be said about lesser institutions other than to condemn them absolutely? It needs to be put on record that Aboriginals throughout Australia *have* been subjected to devastating proselytisation, *have* had their children taken from them on the grounds that as parents they cannot cope (but really this is to speed up the proselytisation process), *have* had their language and ceremonies banned in their own areas, *have* had things like monogamy foisted on them only on the basis that polygamy is sinful, *have* had girls kept in dormitories accompanied by nice little touches like trip-wires and carefully raked sand around buildings so that access and egress tracks can be checked each morning. They *have* been turned into flour, tea and sugar Christians, thus poisoning their health and confusing their minds at the one time. Aboriginal girls *have* been harassed sexually and many of them have been trained for, and then sold into, 'domestic service' which in many cases would have led to further molestation. Jack Davis's fine play *No Sugar* tells the story superbly.

Bullocky's Joy and Jesus

Words and Music: Ted Egan

Calypso Feel

Once upon a time, doing fine
Living in the bush, blackfeller way,
Kids all laughing, Mum and Dad hunting
No worries, no rent to pay.

Then the whitefellers came to stay
Said they'd show us where we went wrong
Said they'd teach us a better way
They taught us to sing a Jesus song.

CHORUS

Bullocky's Joy and Jesus, boy
That's the only way to go
Bullocky's Joy and Jesus, boy,
The Bible tells me so.

Leave the bush, come to the Mission
Can't go naked, much too rude
Girls get dresses, boys get cockrags
Learn to eat the whitefeller food.

Ring the bell, go to school
Teach us all the Golden Rule
Sewing, gardening, everything
And God Save Our Gracious King.

CHORUS

Bullocky's Joy and Jesus, boy etc.

'Line up all you Christian darkies

Manners now! Say 'Thank You' Jacky
Here's your flour, tea and sugar
Bullocky's Joy and black terbaccy'.

Shout 'Hooray' on Blanket Day
That's the day the whitefellers pay
We should be grateful, so they say
Pays for the land they took away.

CHORUS

Bullocky's Joy and Jesus, boy etc.

Guts get fat, teeth all stuffed
Whitefeller tucker make you sick
Social Service, can't go bush
Flagon of plonk might do the trick.

The miners said: 'We'd like this land'.
The Government said: 'We'll give you a hand.
It's Government land, didn't you know
The blackfellers left there long ago'.

CHORUS (TWICE)

Bullocky's Joy and Jesus, boy etc.

There is a happy land, far, far away
Where saints in glory stand, bright, bright as day
No sugar in our tea, bread and butter we
    never see
That's why we're gradually…fading away AMEN.

'Line up all you Christian darkies…' Ration day on a mission station (Photo Department of Aboriginal Affairs)

'Breed Them White'

One of the most sensitive television programs ever presented on Australian television was *Brown Skin Baby*, in which a man of mixed Aboriginal descent rediscovered his mother, a tribal woman from whom he had been taken thirty years previously. His mother was an Anmatjira woman from Central Australia. Bob Randall had been reared as a 'salt water boy' at Croker Island Mission. The sad thing was that they now had nothing in common, other than that they were established as mother and son.

This practice was certainly the worst manifestation of the assimilation policy, whereby officialdom bequeathed unto itself the right to say that those children born of mixed Aboriginal descent would be better off if they were brought up as 'near-whites', encouraged to speak only English, trained along work-ethic lines in the hope that they would not be like those scruffy tribal people who were obviously going to continue to be 'a problem'. On the one hand it was a wonderful way of ridding unscrupulous non-Aboriginals of the embarrassing end results of their promiscuity; on the other hand it backfired absolutely, in that in most cases the children still suffered discrimination, perhaps more, because they could now be labelled 'mongrels' having brown skin rather than black. Little wonder that when it was open to individuals to decide where their identification lay, almost invariably they chose to identify with the Aboriginal side of their heritage, rather than the non-Aboriginal.

Although there are reports of 'children being dragged from the mother's breast' I can only stress that in the latter years of the implementation of the policy, the separation was achieved after a couple of years of persuasion which was called counselling. The mother would then accompany the child to the institution, and regular 'contact visits' were arranged. Thus, re-identification was capable of being achieved reasonably easily when the time came. But for the Bob Randalls, and others who found that their fathers were clergymen, politicians, police, station owners and other 'pillars of society' the scars are deep indeed.

Brown Skin Baby

Words and Music: Bob Randall

Blues feel

A young stockman used to ride
A quiet pony round the countryside
In a native camp he'd never forget
A young black mother, her cheeks all wet.

CHORUS

Yawi, Yawi, my brown skin baby
They takim away.

Between her sobs he heard her say
'Police bin takim my baby away,
'From white man boss that baby I got
'Why he let him take baby away?'

CHORUS

Yawi, Yawi,
My brown skin baby
They takim away.

On a mission station far away
The boy grew up, with a new name
For his mother he searched in vain
Upon this earth they never met again.

CHORUS

Yawi, Yawi,
My brown skin baby
They takim away.

Ngundinadju pulkanu ngura nanagarr
Kaiya pitjala karingu
Ngura parari mulaba
Tjitji abakadja ngaiyu puya kadingu.

CHORUS

Wardju, Wardju,
Tjitji abakadja
Ngaiyu puya kadingu.

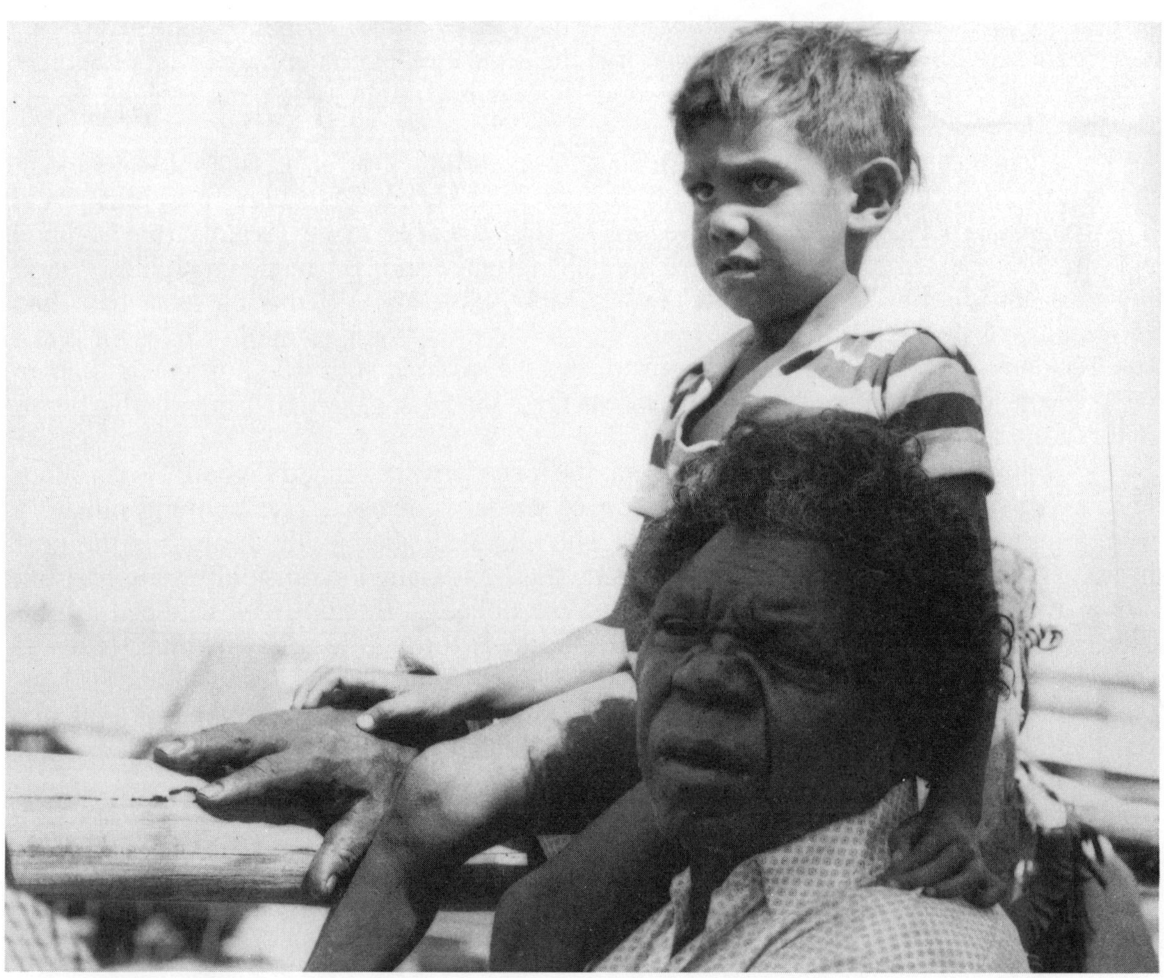

Today's 'brown-skin babies' are usually adopted by tribal foster parents. Musso Harvey of the Yanyula tribe, Borroloola, with his adopted son, Archie (Photo by Allan Howard)

Callous Killer or Freedom Fighter?

History is written by the winners, and from their own perspectives. So most of the history of Australia 1788–1988 has been written by white historians who in most cases could do little better than report that Aboriginals were 'a melancholy footnote to Australian history' or 'a codicil to the real Australian story'.

Thus, Australia has been deprived of any Aboriginal folk heroes. Oh, sure, it's sometimes mentioned that Sam Isaacs was with Grace Bussell when young Grace courageously rode into the Busselton surf to save the survivors. But we know who the real hero was. And sure, the Forrest Brothers erected a headstone over Tommy Winditj's grave at Esperance: they even said he was 'an aborigine (*sic*) of some intelligence'. But the statues are all erected in honour of the great explorers. Sure, we cheered when Evonne Goolagong, the 'joy maker' won Wimbledon, and when Lionel Rose beat Harada. But we were always quick to point out when they lost that it was because of some innate tendency to 'go walkabout' when the chips were down. 'They're like that, you know'. Even Mark Ella came under fire when he found coach Alan Jones too autocratic. 'They can't handle discipline, either'.

To date Aboriginals have not even had the benefit of 'public opinion', that phenomenon which tells the historians they were wrong, that the Kelly Gang were not brutal murderers but 'folk heroes' because the ordinary people say so — so there!

If Yagan had been an escaped Irish convict he would be a household word today, and bearded folk singers would extol his virtues. If Nemarluk was white we'd be as proud of him as we are of Paul Hogan. Don't we look at 'Hoges' and all those larrikins from Gallipoli and think: 'I'm just like that, really. Give me half a chance and I'd wrestle crocodiles, charm the birds and disarm New York with my laid-back Aussie style'. Nemarluk must have had a few laughs as he tracked the police trackers and had them going round in circles for years. And Tuckiar — definitely a Charles Bronson. If the cops hold your wife hostage, and chain her up, you just take them out, man. Boom! One shovel spear, right through the heart, as the cop vainly fires his revolver.

So how will history judge Tjandamara, the man the whites called Pigeon? He is written up in every history of the Kimberley region of Western Australia as a cunning outlaw, a brutal murderer. He was the police tracker who changed sides in 1894, and for the next three years led a bushranging career that made the Kelly Gang look insipid by comparison. He was the man who in his final stand against the police at Tunnel Creek wrapped his .38 calibre ammunition in kangaroo hide in order to fire it through his .45 firearms. He it was who was shot by another Aboriginal — it happened so often. The whites would never have found him on their own. He it was who had his head cut off, to be displayed as evidence that the Western Australian Mounted Police, like their Canadian counterparts, always 'got their man'.

Tjandamara. Callous killer? Freedom fighter?

Tjandamara

Driving rhythm

Chorus
E   B
what do you say a-bout Tjan-da-ma-ra?   What's your o-pin-ion of Che   Ge-va-ra? Were they
E
just - i- fied?________   Have they real-ly died?________
E   B
What do you think a-bout Ro-bin Hood? Could you real-ly call ___ Ned Kel-ly good? And are you
E
sat-is - fied________   when you speak with pride?________   Were they
E
free-dom fight-ers or a - gi-ta - tors?   Blood-y kil-lers or li-ber - a - tors?
C#m   A
Jokes a - side.   It's   the
B
peo-ple who make the   le-gends,   so   let it be cut and dried,____ What's the
B   A   B   E
ver-dict on Tjan-da-ma-ra?________   the peo-ple will de - cide.

54

In April 1897 Australia's whites rejoiced
For the telegram came to say that he was dead
The famous Kimberley outlaw, betrayed and shot
    at last
And as proof the police paraded a severed head.
The white man called him Pigeon
But no-one quite knows why,
Certainly he had a great ability to fly
But his proper name was Tjandamara
Wangarango man of the Tjilia Dreaming
Born and raised in the Kimberley
A hunter through and through.

CHORUS

So what do you say about Tjandamara?
What's your opinion of Che Guevara?
Were they justified? Have they really died?
What did you think about Robin Hood?
Could you really call Ned Kelly 'good'?
And are you satisfied, when you speak with pride?
Were they freedom fighters or agitators?
Bloody killers or liberators?
Jokes aside
It's the people who make the legends
So let it be cut and dried
What's the verdict on Tjandamara?
The people will decide.

He once was a famous tracker for the Kimberley
    police
And he was sent one time to capture a man
A member of his own race.
But the old man told the tracker:

'It's time to make a stand.
Don't be a white man's puppy dog,
Drive the foreigners from your land.'
So he stole the white man's rifles,
Shot the police on sight,
Freed their chained up prisoners in the middle of
    the night
Formed a gang of fighters,
Gave each man a gun
And Tjandamara the tracker
Became an outlaw on the run.

CHORUS

So what do you say etc.

The police brought reinforcements
And trackers by the score
But for three long years he led them a merry
    chase
He tracked their trackers, stole their rifles,
Tunnelled his way through stone,
Until at last he fought them face to face.
There at a place called Tunnel Creek,
He fired his final shot,
And one of his own race killed him,
The ultimate tragic blot.
They took his head in a bag to Derby,
Evidence for the court,
The end of Tjandamara,
Or that was what they thought.

CHORUS

So what do you say etc.

Aboriginal Sporting Stars

Lionel Rose, World Bantamweight Champion (Photo Herald and Weekly Times Ltd)

Elley Bennett, typically mismanaged, but arguably the greatest fighter produced in Australia (Photo News Limited)

A young Doug Nicholls, winner of the 1927 Warracknabeal Gift (Photo Herald and Weekly Times Ltd)

Sir Douglas Nicholls, tireless civil rights worker, first Aboriginal Knight, in London to be knighted by the Queen. He became Governor of South Australia under the Dunstan Government (Photo Herald and Weekly Times Ltd)

Mark Ella, Captain of Australia, one of the all-time greats of World Rugby Union (Photo Herald and Weekly Times Ltd)

Graham (Polly) Farmer typically leaves the opposition flat-footed as he hand-passes to Billy Goggin (Photo Herald and Weekly Times Ltd)

Sport: More Than Equals?

The world has applauded the performances of many Aboriginal sportsmen, and one woman. A visit to the sporting fields in any area of Australia where there are larger than usual numbers of Aboriginals will illustrate that sport is an area where Aboriginals are normally more than equals. One should be wary of generalisations, but it is probably fair to say that most Aboriginals develop better mechanical skills, and at an earlier age, than other Australians. One reason for this is that Aboriginal parents are usually much more permissive in rearing their children. One will see Aboriginal children using axes, handling knives, throwing and catching without constant admonition from parents to 'stop that, you'll get hurt'. The vast majority of Aboriginal children come from poor backgrounds where there are many children who organise their games and leisure around the most basic equipment. We are constantly told that Don Bradman developed his wonderful 'eye' by practising hitting a golf ball against a brick wall with a cricket stump — no mean feat to make contact once, let alone set up a repetitive pattern! The same thing applies with many Aboriginals, to the point where they are usually much better at games and sports requiring natural skills like throwing, dodging and catching than their non-Aboriginal counterparts. The playing fields of Darwin, Katherine, Alice Springs, Cairns, Moree, Kempsey, Port Augusta and Kalgoorlie provide the evidence.

The first Australian cricket team to tour England was entirely composed of Aboriginals. They were from the Edenhope district in Victoria. The tour took place in 1868 (Photo Department of Aboriginal Affairs)

Another generalisation, but probably a valid one, is that Aboriginal girls and women are even better performers than men. So why, then, is Evonne Goolagong Cawley the only Aboriginal woman who can claim top international status? Again, there are important socio-economic factors, like poverty, having children at an earlier age, lack of opportunity etc. But very important too, are the ties to home, and the lack of motivation to be different from one's peers. One wonders what sporting careers might have ensued for some of the wonderful female Aboriginal athletes often seen playing sports like hockey, netball and basketball well into their thirties — but still in the country towns in which they were reared.

If the careers of all the Aboriginal sporting 'greats' are considered, two factors are usually constant — better than average 'natural skills' and a wonderful ability to 'read' the game or the opposition. The question of 'mechanical skills' came to the attention of the English press when reporting the visit of the Aboriginal cricket team to England in 1868. The *Sunday Gazette* of 30 May 1868 reported in awe on the 'native sports' which were demonstrated after each game — things like spear and boomerang throwing, throwing the cricket ball (Dick-a-Dick throwing an amazing 107 yards [98 metres]!); and went on to analyse the fielding skills:

> Their fielding is quite a treat. They throw very well indeed, making the ball whizz along at a great pace…It is very odd to see them catch a ball out in the long field. Every cricketer in England is wont to wait with extended arms and open hand for a coming catch, and then to slightly withdraw his hands to break the force of the ball. But these sturdy Australians adopt the very opposite tactics. When the ball is just passing them, and only then, they make a snatch at it, and generally — nine times out of ten — effect a catch.

Evonne Goolagong, tennis champion (Photo Herald and Weekly Times Ltd)

On the question of ability to 'read' a game or an opponent one only has to consider the careers of 'Polly' Farmer, Maurice Rioli and the Krakouers in Australian football; Arthur Beetson in Rugby League and Mark Ella in Rugby Union; and then to ponder the fact that almost all of the great Australian Aboriginal boxers were counter-punchers.

There was no better counter-puncher than Ron Richards, the subject of my song *The Hungry Fighter*. And there was no more tragic example of the need for proper management and control in the dangerous but exciting sport of boxing.

Ron Richards was born in Ipswich, Queensland in 1910. While in his teens he 'took a glove' in Smalley Higgins' boxing tent, and went on to win three Australian titles (middleweight, light-heavyweight and heavyweight) and the British Empire middleweight title. Along the way he fought and beat the best in the world. In 1938 he knocked out Ray Actis, the number two contender for the world light-heavyweight title, in the first round. In the same year he easily defeated Gus Lesnevitch on points. Lesnevitch went back to America, won the world light-heavyweight title and held it for eight years.

Richards had too many managers, and, consequently, too many fights (142, of which he lost only 19). Instead of being taken in 1938 to fight the world's best his managers kept him in Australia fighting the same opponents time after time — he fought Fred Heneberry ten times, and each was a brutal, brain-scrambling affair. He became involved in some shady affairs where fights were 'thrown' and on one famous occasion Richards propped-up a 'ring-in' for a few rounds before having to knock him out. Richards said later 'The job of holding him up was harder than knocking him down'.

Little wonder that Richards finished up broke and punch-drunk. He hung around the pubs of Darlinghurst and the Haymarket in Sydney, easy prey for the louts who would beat him senseless in order to say 'I K.O.'d Ron Richards'. Too late his plight was made public. He was sent to the Palm Island Aboriginal Reserve in Queensland, hardly a conducive place for rehabilitation. But he spent seventeen years there, growing vegetables, flowers and bananas. 'I grow pretty good bananas', said Richards, a man described by Senator Neville Bonner as 'a steady, sober character, totally uninterested in boxing, and embittered by life's blows.'

Ron Richards eventually returned to Sydney to care for his sick wife, but he was unable to find a job. He died penniless of a heart attack in January 1967. Fred Heneberry took up a collection among old boxers who had known Richards and thus averted a pauper's funeral for the man described by Vic Patrick as the best fighter Australia has ever produced.

The boxing ring attracted many Aboriginal hungry fighters. Lionel Rose was bantamweight champion of the world. Rose, in contrast to Richards, was beautifully managed. Hector Thompson and Tony Mundine both enjoyed world-rated careers, and were well handled. But in the majority of cases the question has to be asked 'How good might he have been if properly trained and managed?' Elley Bennett, Dave Sands. Jack Hassen. How good? Ron Richards?

Ron Richards, the subject of the song The Hungry Fighter. *He held the Australian Middleweight, Light-Heavyweight and Heavyweight titles and the British Empire Middleweight title, but he died penniless and punch-drunk (Photo News Limited)*

The Hungry Fighter

He stood in the dusty showground
Of every country town you've ever known
He'd come in from the mission
Sixteen years of age but fully grown
He had a shilling to spend
So he bought a pie
It was then that he caught the showman's eye
At the boxing tent on a platform high
And another hungry fighter was on his way
Yes another hungry fighter was on his way.

Hear the big bass drum
See the yokels come,
'Will you take a glove?' that's what the showman
    said.
'You might make a quid
'Wadda ya say there kid?
'You'll fight the Killer?
'Have you got rocks in your head?
'Don't you know that the killer's a professional,
    son?

'And you say you're not insured?
'But step on up, you're a likely lad,
And the Killer will knock your block off, rest
    assured.
'The Killer will knock your block off, rest
    assured.'

'Rollup, roll up, ladies and gentlemen, for the big
    boxing show, starting here, in the tent, any
    moment. This young darkie here has dared
    to challenge the Killer. We have the
    ambulance standing by. Get your tickets at
    the ticket box. Show starting — soon.'

Well, The Killer was a tired old has-been
And even though the referee tried his best
The Kid soon flattened the old bloke,
Two left hooks and a right cross did the rest.
So they signed him up and he joined the show
Three fights a day, what a way to go
But it was better than school, he was earning
    dough

And another hungry fighter was on his way
Yes another hungry fighter was on his way.

They took him down to the city
And pretty soon he was fighting main events
Fancy suits and taxi cabs
He'd come a long way since he left the boxing
    tents
And was he good? Best in the land,
With a knockout punch in either hand
And a walk-up style that they couldn't withstand
Yes the hungry fighter was really on his way
The hungry fighter was really on his way.

Well, he won the national title
So his managers brought in stars from overseas
Rough stuff, but he was gutsy
And one by one he demolished all of these
But he took such punishment in each fight
It scrambled his brains, impaired his sight,
The managers said: 'Kid, you'll be right'.
But the hungry fighter was on the way downhill.
The hungry fighter was on the way downhill.

He lost his national title
But the managers matched him time and time
    again
Soon he gave up training
Found a couple of drinks would help to ease the
    pain
The managers all stayed rich and fat
They bought him a guitar and a cowboy hat
And then a second-rater knocked him flat,
And the doctor said: 'Son, give the game away'
'Hungry fighter, give the game away'.

Hear the big bass drum

See the yokels come
'Will you take a glove?' that's what the showman
    said.
'Here's a jackeroo
'What's your name son? Blue?
'You'll fight the Champ?
'Have you got rocks in your head?
'Don't you know that the Champ beat the Yankee
    bloke?
'Present world title holder?
'But come on up, Blue, you're a likely lad,
'I've never ever ever seen one bolder
'No I've never ever, ever seen one bolder'.

'Rollup, roll up ladies and gentlemen, for the big
    boxing show starting here, in the tent, any
    moment. Young Blue here, the jackeroo, has
    dared to challenge The Champ, the greatest
    Aboriginal boxer this country has ever seen.
    Blue, son, do you believe in suicide? But get
    your tickets at the ticket box. Show starting
    — soon.'

He shuffled through the Sydney markets
Puffed-up face, no shoes upon his feet
Checked out all the rubbish tins,
Then a kind old lady gave him a bite to eat.
He'd been bashed last night in Redfern Park
By a gang of thugs lurking in the dark
And one of these was heard to remark:
'That old boong was once a fighter so they say,
That old boong was once a fighter so they say'.
And the hungry fighter faces another day.

Hear the big bass drum —
'Would you take a glove?' that's what the
    showman said…

The Assimilation Policy and Its Victims

Albert Namatjira is of course internationally famous for the vivid way in which he painted Central Australia's starkly beautiful landscapes. He is usually written up as a tragic figure, a man 'between two worlds'. There are many people who knew Namatjira better than I, but I did have some contact with him, both in Darwin, where he stayed for a week at my house prior to going to meet the Queen in 1954, and in Central Australia in the few years prior to his death in 1959. I would certainly not apply the word 'tragic' to Albert Namatjira in the same way that I would apply it to Ron Richards — the subject of my song *The Hungry Fighter*. In searching for a single adjective to describe Albert Namatjira only one comes to mind: dignified. In fact he was the most dignified person I ever met, dignified almost to the point of the aloofness which the British aristocracy publicly project. A 'more quiet man altogether' is how Aboriginals would describe him.

The story that evolved around Namatjira is truly a tragic one, and, as I worked for the Commonwealth Government Department which administered its Aboriginal policies at the time I must take on some of the collective guilt.

We now have the wisdom of hindsight about the assimilation policy, but in 1931, when it was first mooted, it seemed to be the first positive policy ever envisaged for Aboriginals. Following the last two official massacres of Aboriginals in 1928 at Coniston and 1931 at Forrest River there was international concern expressed about the way in which Australia's Aboriginals were slowly but surely being eliminated. People like Daisy Bates had proposed that the best that could be done was to 'smooth the pillow of a dying race'. Professor A.P. Elkin and others proposed an approach whereby some reserves would be created for tribal people, and that other Aboriginal people should be educated, clothed, housed, and generally taught to use and appreciate the benefits of 'civilisation' to the point where they would see the advantages of 'being like us' in one big, happy, English-speaking Australian community.

Reserves like Arnhem Land were created, and some very questionable practices, like taking mixed-race children from their tribal mothers in order that they could be educated at institutions, were implemented. But none of the positive things envisaged by Elkin and others were to come to pass until the appointment of Paul (later Sir Paul, Governor-General of Australia) Hasluck to the portfolio of Minister for Territories in the early 1950s. Hasluck, an eminent scholar who had written very sympathetic books about the plight of Aboriginals, was not your typical minister. He was more like a permanent head of a Department, particularly in his wish to promote a better physical scenario for Aboriginals. Hasluck's approach was certainly different. He sought to have The Aboriginals Ordinance in the Northern Territory repealed absolutely on the grounds that it discriminated against Aboriginals purely and simply on the basis of race. He sought to replace it with a Welfare Ordinance, whereby assistance could be given to 'certain persons' on the grounds mainly of 'their inability without assistance adequately to manage their own affairs'. Those 'certain persons' would be called 'wards' within the meaning of the Ordinance.

No points for guessing who the 'certain persons' were. The old Aboriginals Ordinance was repealed; and the most important ramification was that, at that point, all 'part-Aboriginals' — except for a few who were living tribal lives — were thereby exempted from all discriminatory legislation. They were now free, 'like us'. But at the same time the new Welfare Ordinance was introduced. In the two years preceding this legislative change all members of the staff of the Native Affairs Branch, as it was then called in the Northern Territory, had been prepar-

Albert Namatjira escorting Dame Mary Gilmore in 1956 (Photo by Hopwood, Sydney Morning Herald*)*

ing a most comprehensive census of all 'full-blood' Aboriginals. A census book was compiled — quickly called the 'stud book' by cynics, who also made the predictable 'jokes' like: 'We musn't call them boongs any more, oh, no, they're our precious little wards'. In one legislative stroke the Welfare Ordinance (1954) was implemented and those persons 'deemed to be in need of assistance' were included in the Register of Wards. Basically the laws were the same. Just as 'Aboriginals' had not been allowed to vote, drink liquor, live in towns, marry without permission etc., now 16,000 'wards' all of whom were 'full-blooded' or 'tribal' Aboriginals were in basically the same discriminatory situation. But now the basis of discrimination lay not in race, but in declared social need. It is important to note that no non-Aboriginals were declared wards.

Clever stuff. A rose by any other name. A minor administrative snag lay in the fact that there were a few tribal Aboriginals who very definitely could 'manage their own affairs' and who clearly did not 'stand in need of assistance'. Albert Namatjira was one. He had for many years been earning big money from the sales of his paintings. He owned a block of land in town — but was not allowed to build on it. He owned motor cars, and distributed tribal largesse among his relations as he was bound to do. So Albert Namatjira was not declared to be a 'ward'. All of his family were. They were wards: he was a 'person other than a ward'.

One of the sections of the Welfare Ordinance ordained that it was an offence if 'any person was found guilty of supplying intoxicating liquor to a ward'. The penalty was a mandatory six months imprisonment. The police waited with unconcealed delight as Namatjira purchased a bottle of wine and then 'illegally' shared it with his family. Officialdom had egg on its face as this internationally-known celebrity received his six months sentence in stony silence.

The wily Hasluck spotted the political implications. He quickly had the Haast Bluff Aboriginal reserve gazetted as an 'institution within the meaning of the N.T. Prisons Ordinance'. Namatjira was whisked out of sight, out of town, out of contact with journalists and photographers, to spend the next six months not incarcerated in a prison, but committed to an Aboriginal Reserve.

On appeal, Namatjira's sentence was reduced to three months. In fact he served only eight weeks committal, with remission for good behaviour. He was released in May 1959 and returned to Hermannsburg. He seemed to have lost the will to live or to paint. He had a heart attack and died on 8 August 1959.

His burial service was conducted at the Alice Springs Cemetery by his old friend Pastor Albrecht. His wife, Rubina, was the principal mourner.

Albert Namatjira

Words and Music: Ted Egan

Strong, driving rhythm

Sitting in the dirt
And the trial is finally done
I'm to spend six months in gaol
Just for sharing with my son.

When I was young I walked this land
With wise old men who said:
'When we change you to a man,
'If you don't share, you're dead'.

I endured the great ordeal
Promised to obey the rules
Vital desert laws that teach
Better than the white man's schools.

CHANT

Albert Namatjira, Albert Namatjira

I learnt to paint the white man's way
I learnt that I must keep my place
They wanted me to meet their Queen
Tokenism for my race.

Then they split my family up
With their tricky white man laws
Waited for me, then they pounced,
Clang the closing prison doors.

CHANT

Albert Namatjira, Albert Namatjira

As I sit here in the dust
I think of how I've known this land
Legends of my ancestors
No more will flow from painter's hand.

I sit and think my ancient thoughts
An old man's memory
Take me to your prison now
Leave me with my dignity.

CHANT

Albert Namatjira, Albert Namatjira

'If You Were White...'

Probably my most vivid memory of my early years in Darwin is to recall the sight of an old Aboriginal woman named Alyandabu who used to walk into town each day. She had the erect, graceful carriage achieved by many Aboriginal women as a result of being trained to carry things on the head, thus leaving their hands free to gather food. She was almost six feet tall, and, again like many other Aboriginal women of the period, smoked a pipe. Usually she wore a wide-brimmed hat, either felt or straw panama. She was often barefooted, wore simple cotton frocks, and carried a few items tied in a red handkerchief. She could have walked straight out of a Russell Drysdale canvas.

Alyandabu was called Alyan by other Aboriginals, Wetji by members of her family, and Lucy McGinness by the non-Aboriginal people of Darwin. She was one of the few survivors of the Khungarakung tribe whose members had been given poisoned flour by early white intruders into their country. Yet Alyandabu was later to meet and marry a white man, an Irishman named Stephen McGinness, and raise a fine family of four sons and a daughter. The relationship between Alyandabu and Stephen McGinness was quite extraordinary for the times. Today, their many descendants throughout Australia are fiercely proud of their unique Aboriginal/Irish/Australian heritage, and especially fond of the memory of the matriarch who died in 1961 at the age of eighty-six.

Alyandabu and Stephen McGinness lived and worked in railway fettler camps on the old North Australia railway. Then they found the rich Lucy tin mine and worked it together, at the same time rearing their family and teaching their children all the things they would need to know if they were to retain their identity. The children were all thoroughly educated in both the Aboriginal and western sense. Two sons especially, Joe and Jack, were in the forefront of the national Aboriginal rights movement long before it was fashionable.

Following Stephen McGinness's untimely death Alyandabu was confronted by the realisation that in legal terms she was an alien in her own country. Her mine was forfeited, and she was instructed to go to Darwin where her younger children were to be taken into the Aboriginal compound. She had to engage in arduous physical jobs in Darwin in order to be near her children. When the children grew up the family was able to be reunited in Darwin, where Alyandabu lived until her death.

In standard Australian terms Alyandabu's was a straightforward pioneering life, tough in the living, admirable in retrospect, the stuff of which books and films are made. Towns, streets, parks and buildings in this country have been named after much lesser beings. I hope that one of Alyandabu's descendants will do her justice by writing a detailed biography.

'Straight out of a Drysdale canvas you walked…'; Alyandabu by Robert Ingpen

Alyandabu

Gentle country feel
Words and Music: Ted Egan
Verse
C
Straight out of a Drys - dale can-vas you walked, Down Ves-tey's Hill past the
C   G7
Gov -ern-ment Gar-dens, And right on in - to town
G
Straight as a spear shaft, wide brimmed hat tall and proud and black. It's just
G7   C   Chorus
one of the ma-ny roads that you've walked down. And I
F   F   C
won-der what you're think-ing a-bout, As you walk on through your life. Are you
F   D7   G
think-ing a-bout the Ir - ish - man who took you as his wife? Or the
C   Am   D   G7
kids you bore? the things you saw? The hard times you were made to en-dure What's your
C   C   G   C
sto -ry? Al - yan - da-bu.

Straight out of a Drysdale canvas you walked
Down Vestey's Hill
Past the Government Gardens
And right on into town
Straight as a spear shaft
Wide-brimmed hat
Tall and proud and black
It's just one of the many roads that you've walked
    down.

CHORUS

And I wonder what you're thinking about
As you walk on through your life
Are you thinking about the Irishman
Who took you as his wife?
Or the kids you bore?
The things you saw?
The hard times you were made to endure?
What's your story?
Alyandabu.

When you were young you saw your people killed
Your tribe cut down
Poisoned flour and bullets were their fate
But you survived
And in your life
A laughing Irishman arrived
And you both shared a life that knew no hate.

You found the famous Lucy Mine
Worked it with your man
Raised five kids but then disaster came
McGinniss died
Officials tried
To take your children from you
They wanted both your family and your claim.

Into Darwin town you came
Fighting for your rights
Working to keep your family by your side
Today you'd be so fond of them
Descendants by the score
You taught them all about a thing called pride.

So I wonder what your memories are
As you walk by
Waving to your friends along the way?
As you serenely smoke your pipe
Knowing all you know
You represent a life that's gone today.

If you were white they'd call you a pioneer
Name a suburb after you
Yet you're forgotten by the ones who took your
    land
But those who've known you, known your worth
Cherish private thoughts
Memories strangers wouldn't understand.

Land Rights

'Let it not be said the fair equitable recognition of Aboriginal rights to land is discrimination. To call for the acknowledgement of the land rights of people who have never surrendered those rights is not discrimination. Certainly, what has been done cannot be undone. But what can now be done to remedy the deeds of yesterday must not be put off till tomorrow.'

Pope John Paul II, speaking at Alice Springs 1986

If the Yirrkala Aboriginals lost the legal battle for their land in 1970, the Gurindji can be said to have won probably the most important Aboriginal political struggle in Australian history when they were accorded title over some of their traditional land in 1973. When the more definitive histories of Australia are written many a Prime Minister may be overlooked but Vincent Lingiari will not.

Vincent Lingiari was a clan leader among the Gurindji tribe whose lands had been alienated (although the Gurindji were not told of this) when pastoral leases were granted to white settlers in the 1880s. First to bring cattle to Wave Hill Station, as the country came to be called, was Nat Buchanan, the famous drover. Buchanan ran the station for a few years, followed by his brother Frank, and then the station was taken over by company interests. By 1914 the huge Vestey Empire in England had acquired the station.

As with most other of the vast northern cattle stations a typical feudal set-up was established. As far as Aboriginals were concerned those prepared to compromise with the fact that the whites were in charge were employed in various capacities: those who did not conform were either shot or driven off.

Young Aboriginal ringers (stockmen) at the Daly Waters rodeo (NT) (Photo by Allan Howard)

Work on the station consisted of stockwork for the men (and the women in the early days) and domestic service for the women. The large number of part-Aboriginal children born at places like Wave Hill is indicative of the levels of miscegenation and prostitution which occurred, sometimes with Aboriginal concurrence, but always on the basis that the Aboriginals, tied spiritually to their land, had no option other than to accept whatever treatment the whites dished out.

Because of their complete lack of interest in the Aboriginals on cultural grounds the whites made no attempt to interfere with the ceremonial life of the Gurindji, who retained their ceremonies, their language and their laws during what was called 'the walkabout season' — that time when there is no cattle work to be done and whites assume that Aboriginals walk aimlessly around the bush.

Although life was feudal and sometimes barbaric the Gurindji were luckier than many other groups: at least they survived, and with pride intact. Stockwork was a challenge to use local knowledge and the unique bush skills, like tracking, which are an integral part of the traditional Aboriginal life. Basic foodstuffs like beef and flour were usually available, and living in their own country meant that the Gurindji still had access to their traditional bush foods. The very nature of stockwork made it possible for them to retain custodianship of the land in Aboriginal terms, and they obviously did not tell the whites the significance of some of the areas. In years to come, of course, they would be accused of 'inventing' sacred sites.

Life was thus, from the 1880s to the 1950s. The adults worked hard and well, most were reasonably healthy, and the fact that they were paid no cash wages was not quite as criminal as it might be made to seem. The year 1953 was something of a milestone, for that year the Gurindji stockmen all received the first 'cash longa finger' they had ever been paid in seventy years of serfdom: each stockman was given a £5 note to spend at the Negri Races.

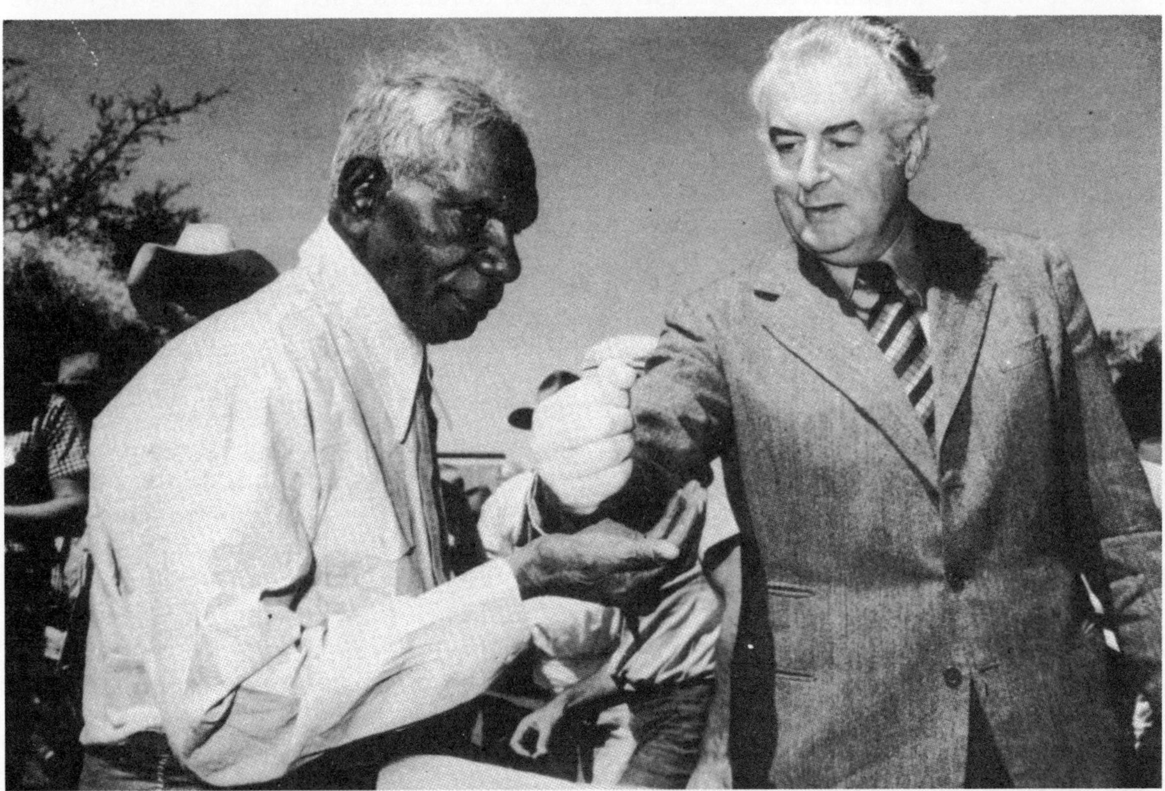

Gough Whitlam, then Prime Minister of Australia, passes a handful of soil to Vincent Lingiari in the first recognition of traditional ownership of land by Aboriginals in Australia ever to be made, 1973 (Photo Department of Aboriginal Affairs)

And then, in August 1966, to the amazement of everybody in the district, a group of two hundred Gurindji people walked off Wave Hill Station, led by Vincent Lingiari, to set up a camp twenty miles away at a place they called Daguragu, but which white people called Wattie Creek. The Gurindji said, simply, that they were 'tired of being pushed around like dogs'. First reports of the walk-off were greeted with little short of mirth in Government and pastoral circles: it was felt that the Gurindji would 'come to their senses when they ran out of tucker'. But an Aboriginal union organiser named Dexter Daniels reported the facts to the Darwin office of the North Australian Workers Union in Darwin, and union leaders arranged for a truckload of food to be sent 500 miles [800 kilometres] to the Gurindji. Daniels and others were blamed for the whole affair and branded as 'Communist stirrers' and moves were made to prevent them entering the Wave Hill lease which still included Daguragu. Union officials had legal access, however, and the food supplies were continued. A local welfare officer, Bill Jeffreys, sympathetic to the Gurindji, was transferred from the area.

The Gurindji said that they were sick of being 'slaves' and wanted to set up their own cattle station with Daguragu as its headquarters. This was heresy indeed. But the trade union movement, and ABSCHOL, a University student union movement, together with writer Frank Hardy, took up the Gurindji cause and arranged for Vincent Lingiari, Donald Nangiari and Captain Major to talk to university campuses and union meetings. Their basic honesty and the modest extent of their aspirations could not help but impress.

It was heady stuff. The battler takes on the big fellow. Demonstrations of thousands of Gurindji supporters were organised outside Vestey headquarters in the capital cities, and the expression 'land rights' was heard in Australia for the first time. There is a story, possibly true, that a young girl parading with a 'LAND RIGHTS FOR THE GURINDJI' banner was accosted by a heckler. 'You wouldn't know a Gurindji from a barramundi' the heckler was alleged to have said. 'I don't care,' the girl is alleged to have replied, 'as long as they both get their land rights.'

The Gurindji leaders were fêted, and students and other supporters went with Hardy to Wattie Creek to work. The unions collected $10,000 for the purchase of fencing materials and some horses. Hardy wrote a popular book, *The Unlucky Australians*, whereupon he and the other supporters were branded as 'southern communist stirrers' — the ultimate disacclaim in frontier Australia. The Commonwealth Government built an entire township at what was called Wave Hill township (now Kalkaringi) but the Gurindji resisted the dangled carrot. The fifteen three-bedroom brick houses with all modern conveniences remained empty for some months while the Gurindji built bough sheds for themselves at Daguragu. Later the houses at Kalkaringi were occupied by other Aboriginals.

There was hostile debate within Government ranks about how to resolve this and other Aboriginal issues. There were two Commonwealth bodies each of the opinion that it was the official body representing the Government in Aboriginal Affairs. One was the Office of Aboriginal Affairs, led by the redoubtable Dr H.C. 'Nugget' Coombs. The other was the Department of the Interior which had as its Minister the Country Party stalwart Peter Nixon and as its principal Northern Territory spokesman Mr Harry Giese, the implementer of the Hasluck-inspired assimilation policy. The Office of Aboriginal Affairs supported the Gurindji in their land rights claims. The Department of the Interior felt that the Government township at Kalkaringi would provide the proper amenities for any Aboriginals who did not wish to continue employment at Wave Hill Station.

I was employed by the Office of Aboriginal Affairs and, along with Phillip Roberts (the subject of the book *I the Aboriginal*), became heavily involved in the Gurindji struggle. I was moved to write my song 'Gurindji Blues' on the night of 9 September 1969 after Peter Nixon, Minister for the Interior — who was paid a handsome salary to look after the best interests of Aboriginals — said in Parliament that if the Gurindji wanted land they should save up and buy it, just as any other good Australian would. When the recorded version of the song was released, introduced by a short, historic statement by Vincent Lingiari, the

Secretary of Nixon's Department in Canberra rang Dr Coombs to demand that I be sacked from the Public Service. Dr Coombs replied that he rather liked the song, and felt it was a fairly succinct appraisal of what had transpired.

The Gurindji held out, bought a few cattle and horses, built stockyards, erected some symbolic fencing, and gradually formalised their claim to a sizeable proportion of the Wave Hill lease — enough 'to run a cattle station'. The Holt, Gorton and McMahon Governments all refused to recognise their claims.

In England Lord Vestey saw the electoral writing on the wall. It was fairly obvious that Whitlam and Labor would win the next election. As a token recognition of the moral obligations mentioned by Justice Blackburn in the *Yirrkala 'land rights' case*, Prime Minister McMahon proposed on Australia Day 1972 giving leases over some Aboriginal reserves to the Aboriginal groups living thereon. Vestey quickly wrote to McMahon offering to surrender half the Wave Hill lease — an area of around 1250 square miles [3250 square kilometres] and certainly 'enough to run a cattle station' — in order that a lease might be given to the Gurindji. McMahon ignored the offer.

The McMahon Government was defeated in December 1972 and the Whitlam Government quickly granted the Gurindji a lease over what is now called Daguragu cattle station. Vestey was paid at market value. Whitlam went personally to Daguragu and symbolically passed to Vincent Lingiari a handful of soil and the title deeds to Daguragu. This situation was enhanced in 1986 when the title over the land was converted to inalienable Aboriginal Title under the Land Rights Act.

Today, the Gurindji are alive and well. They may not be the greatest pastoralists in the world, although they are doing well enough, but they are secure on their own land forever, and largely organising their own lives according to their own needs and aspirations. They forgive easily, and their relationships with all whites are amazingly cordial.

Gurindji Blues

Words and Music: Ted Egan

Moderately fast

Poor bugger me, Gurindji
Me bin sit down this country
Long time before the Lord Vestey
Allabout land belongin' to we
Oh poor bugger me, Gurindji.
Poor bugger blackfeller, Gurindji
Long time work no wages, we,
Work for the good old Lord Vestey
Little bit flour, sugar and tea
For the Gurindji, from Lord Vestey
Oh poor bugger me.

Poor bugger me, Gurindji,
Man called Vincent Lingiari
Talk long allabout Gurindji
'Daguragu place for we,
Home for we, Gurindji'.
But poor bugger blackfeller, Gurindji
Government boss him talk long we
'We'll build you house with electricity
But at Wave Hill, for can't you see
Wattie Creek belong to Lord Vestey'
Oh poor bugger me.

Poor bugger me, Gurindji
Up come Mr. Frank Hardy
ABSCHOL too and talk long we
Givit hand long Gurindji
Buildim house and plantim tree
Longa Wattie Creek for Gurindji
But poor bugger blackfeller Gurindji
Government Law him talk long we
'Can't givit land long blackfeller, see
Only spoilim Gurindji'
Oh poor bugger me.

Poor bugger me, Gurindji
Peter Nixon talk long we:
'Buy you own land, Gurindji
Buyim back from the Lord Vestey'
Oh poor bugger me, Gurindji.
Poor bugger blackfeller Gurindji
Suppose we buyim back country
What you reckon proper fee?
Might be flour, sugar and tea
From the Gurindji to Lord Vestey?
Oh poor bugger me.

Oh ngaiyu luyurr ngura-u
Sorry my country, Gurindji.

*Pincher Numiari, head stockman for the
Gurindji cattle station at Daguragu (NT)*

Aboriginal Land in Australia

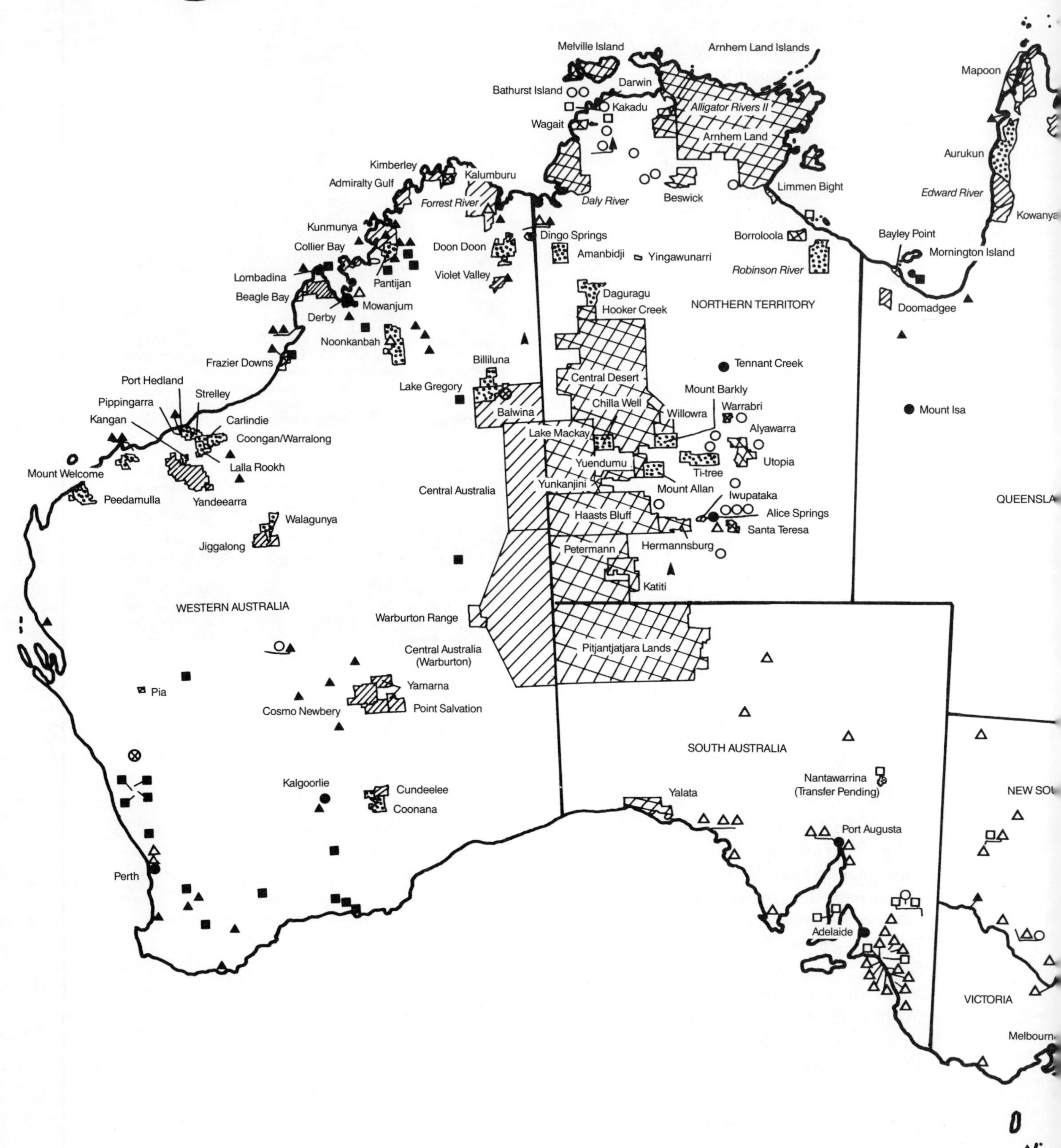

Adapted from map and information in Department of Aboriginal Affairs, *Aboriginals in Australia Today*

Aboriginal land and population in Australia

State	Land							Population		
	Aboriginal Freehold (km²)	Aboriginal Leasehold (km²)	Aboriginal Reserves (km²)	Aboriginal Missions (km²)	Total Aboriginal Land (km²)	Total Land Area (km²)	Aboriginal Proportion of Land (%)	Aboriginal Population Dec. 1981(a)	Total Population Dec. 1981	Aboriginal Proportion of Total Population (%)
N.S.W.—A.C.T.	152	121	—	—	273	804 000	0.03	36 190	5 464 400	0.66
Vic.	20	—	—	—	20	227 600	0.01	9 057	3 948 600	0.15
Qld.	5	8 721	21 344	—	30 070	1 727 200	1.74	44 698	2 345 300	1.91
S.A.	106 763	506	—	—	107 269	984 000	10.90	9 825	1 319 300	0.74
W.A.	9	25 708	192 422	649	218 788	2 525 000	8.66	31 351	1 299 100	2.41
Tas	1	—	—	—	1	67 800	0.001	2 688	427 300	0.63
N.T.	362 930	26 759	—	42	389 731	1 346 200	28.95	29 088	122 800	23.69
Aust.	469 880	61 815	213 766	691	746 152	7 682 300	9.71	159 897	14 926 800	1.07

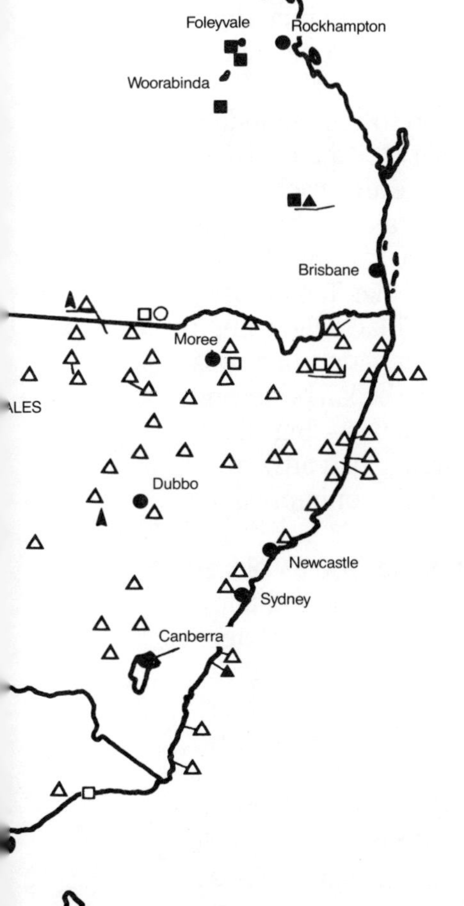

Tenure		Area (hectares)		
		10-1000	1000-10 000	>10 000
Freehold*	Freehold or leasehold land held by Aboriginal land trusts; the Aboriginal Development Commission or incorporated Aboriginal groups. Excludes land held privately by Aboriginals.	△	☐	(crosshatch)
Leasehold		○	▲	(dotted)
Reserve	Crown land reserved for Aboriginals. Excludes archaeological and historic sites.	▲	■	(hatched)
Mission	Freehold or leasehold land held by church groups for Aboriginal missions.	⊕	⊞	(solid black)

*Includes all land claims approved by the Minister under the
Aboriginal Land Rights (Northern Territory) Act 1976 as at 30.6.82.

A Question of Identity

I wrote my song *Poor Feller My Country** one night after I had been asked to convene a meeting of old tribal Aboriginals in Darwin. My brief at the meeting was to find out how they felt their people were faring in the face of the frenzied economic activity, mainly mining exploration, which was going on in their respective areas. To my surprise, and in the face of what seemed to me to be incontrovertible evidence that most of them were being sold down the drain by the Government which purported to be acting in their best interests, they were unanimous in their belief that things were fine, just fine. I wondered whether I had the right to disenchant them, and decided that I didn't.

It seemed to me that their ties with the land were so close they felt a false sense of security, a feeling that they were invulnerable. In former times this would be true. As long as they did not disabuse their totemic affiliations nothing could go wrong. The land and all its creatures were one: the ultimate in identity and identification. I had heard so many Aboriginals greet one another in English by saying 'Gooday country'. Now I knew the extent of the greeting. You are not just my countryman: you are my country and I am yours. It would be a couple of years later when Justice Blackburn said in the Yirrkala case that 'the Aboriginals don't own the land, but the land owns them'. That is why in the song the old man does not say 'This is your country'. Instead he says: 'This you country'. One and the same.

I didn't sleep much that night, pondering the various elements which constitute a total identity. I have always admired the Welsh, who have retained their language, their personal and place names and their pride in their history and traditions in the face of incredible persecution by the English. I had often thought that if I was an Aboriginal I would refuse to speak anything other than my own language: let the foreigners learn Australian. The problem for so many Aboriginals is that their willingness to be friendly, and to accommodate whites, has led to the sort of attenuation of identity that make it unnecessary for the usurpers to impose laws and implement prohibitions: Aboriginals have fallen for every trick that's ever been played in the loss of identity stakes. Assertive whites have created institutions and conned Aboriginals into giving up hunting and foraging in exchange for rations of flour, tea and sugar. Whites who have no trouble coming to terms with names like Tchaikovsky and McGillicuddy will impose English names on Aboriginals because 'that blackfellow lingo is too rough'. I listened in dismay once when the chairman of a mining company which was operating on an Aboriginal reserve, looked expansively around him and blandly began bestowing place names like Town Beach, Wallaby Beach (he had seen a wallaby there — big deal!) and — wait for it — Point Pleasant. When I pointed out that the places already had attractive, centuries-old names like Birritjimi, Burulilipa and Lormbuwoy he was singularly unimpressed. And guess whose place names are now in use.

What's in a name? Plenty. Ridiculous and proprietary personal names are as old as serfdom. It is nothing short of tragic to see particularly tribal Aboriginals sit back and allow whites to bestow anglicised names on them, especially when the sinister Queensland pattern — based on the old 'master-boy' American slave days — is applied, and children are given the first name of their fathers as their surname. So people finish up with names like Mary Dick and Susan Tom. Who is going to treat Susan Tom as anything other than a joke? And what of the station owner whose love for the Sport of Kings caused him to name one of his pet blacks Phar Lap and then bestow the names Bernborough, Todman and Shannon on the man's three sons? Actually the shortened names Bernie, Toddy and Shannon weren't too bad in the final analysis, but it leads people into games of one-upmanship.[†] Those Aboriginals who have had ridiculous or unsatisfactory names foisted on them should do what Muhammud Ali did: he cast aside the slave-name Cassius Clay as though throwing chains away. There is probably not one Aboriginal in Australia for whom a meaningful Aboriginal name could not be worked out.

On the question of language, it is sad that most Aboriginals have lost their original languages forever. But there are languages written down, recorded and capable of being learnt by anybody who really cares about identity. The biggest problem for many urbanised Aboriginals, and especially activists, is that to knuckle down to the hard grind of learning languages and other things about Aboriginals which must be learned academically, like anthropology, is to acknowledge a deficiency in that which gets them in front of the media, that which gives them their place in the sun — their Aboriginality. But they would be more convincing Aboriginals.

*Written many years before Xavier Herbert's book

†I must not absolve myself from blame. At Yuendumu once there was a little boy named Billy Jambijinba. He was a fat, jolly little bloke and I nicknamed him Billy Bunter. Several years later in Darwin I was accosted by a tall, slim young Aboriginal man. 'Remember me?' he asked. I had to acknowledge that I didn't. 'I'm a schoolteacher now' he said. 'Billy Bunter'.

Mithinari, a famous artist from Arnhem Land. Such people are so secure in their own worlds that they are totally vulnerable to the outside world

Poor Feller My Country

Words and Music: Ted Egan

Fast 3 (slow 1 per bar)

Once when I'm young boy
Old man tell me
'Always look after
This you country.
You are a river
You are the sea
You are the rocks, boy,
This you country.'

CHORUS

Poor feller my country
Poor feller me
Dreaming's a nightmare
Poor feller me.

Once in a Dreamtime
Happy and free
People of nature
In our country
I was an emu
Red kangaroo
Dance in the firelight
Didgeridoo.

CHORUS

Poor feller my country etc.

Civilisation

Work for the boss
Put on some clothes, boy,
Cover your loss
I was a moonbeam
Star in the sky
I was the lightning
Flashing on high.

CHORUS

Poor feller my country etc.

Talk to the tourists
Shop at the store
Mining uranium
Money galore
I am a bottle
I am a can
Wrapped up in plastic
Civilised man.

CHORUS

Poor feller my country
Poor feller me
Dreaming's a nightmare
Poor feller me.
Dreaming's a nightmare
Poor feller me.

We'll Tell the Story

I wanted to include Ernie Dingo's song *King Wally* in this book and on the album *The Aboriginals* for two reasons. Firstly, it is a very good song. Secondly, it is an indicator that we will hear the Aboriginal 'message', the contemporary based on the traditional, coming through loud and clear from Aboriginals themselves from now on. We are used to this through political action, demonstrations and the like. But remember the statement of the Irish poet Thomas Moore: 'I care not who makes the laws of this country, as long as I write the songs'. It is arguable that Dylan Thomas and James Baldwin have done more to promote awareness of the feelings and aspirations of their own minorities than did any politicians. The start for Aboriginals was made by Colin Johnston, Kath Walker, Kevin Gilbert and Jack Davis. Today there are many involved, creative young people who are articulate, aware, and proud of their Aboriginality.

So are non-Aboriginals barred from comment? They should not be. It's a relatively free country, and I would argue that the more dialogue the better. I feel both relaxed about, and qualified to write about Aboriginals, from a non-Aboriginal perspective. And for what it is worth I would like to put down a few hopefully objective observations probably implicit in my songs but perhaps not specific. So many issues are clouded, misconstrued and obfuscated by politics and politicians. What the country needs is a practical, humane, multi-lateral policy courageously implemented. If we do not come to terms with these important issues in all sections of Australian society we may expect nothing better than to have all Aboriginals with a chip on the shoulder, and demanding compensation and retribution for ever. They will say we owe it to them: the rest of the world will say it serves us right.

These points may be worthy of consideration:

1) There should be a well-prepared, authentic and attractively presented campaign in all schools to demonstrate the extent and nature of the Aboriginal occupancy of this continent pre-1788, juxtaposed alongside today's situation. Given that nowadays all news is bad news about brutality, terrorism, war and the mindless ravaging of nature even in Australia, children may be only too happy to develop pride in the fact that the traditional Aboriginal lifestyle is conservative, conservationist and peaceful. Unbiased history and simple language courses should be introduced at the earliest suitable age.

2) Just as monuments are erected to honour soldiers from various wars and prominent figures in society, throughout Australia there should be a carefully orchestrated campaign endorsed by eminent Australians to seek to promote more enlightened attitudes in the community. Regrettably, the vast majority of non-Aboriginals know nothing about Aboriginals, yet feel free to hold contemptuous, racist and ill-informed attitudes. This suits the politicians, for there are no votes in positive thinking about Aboriginals, but plenty in Aboriginal bashing. The same politicians will blatantly suggest to Australians that they are the world's champions at getting a fair deal for the underdog.

3) The Commonwealth does have legal power both to legislate in general terms for Aboriginals (Section 51 (xxvi) of the Constitution) and also 'to acquire property on just terms from any state or person for any purpose in respect of which the Parliament has power to make laws'. (Section 51 (xxxi) of the Constitution). It should, where necessary, use these powers on two quite different levels — to grant 'traditional Aboriginal land title' in appropriate areas, and 'Aboriginal land title' in areas where there is no ongoing ceremonial connection but nonetheless an Aboriginal presence.

4) Only where Aboriginal people still retain their language, perform ceremonies and observe traditional laws should 'traditional Aboriginal land rights' be recognised. They must necessarily be relatively large areas, given that people need to be largely undisturbed if this is their wish. The needs of the entire nation could be resolved in five years, and at that point it would be surprising how little anybody was affected, other than beneficially (in the case of the Aboriginals concerned) for we are only talking about Central and northern Australia.

5) In areas where tribal traditions are no longer observed, but cohesive, recognisable Aboriginal groups are identified as separate social units, property should if necessary be arbitrarily purchased on their behalf. And no strings should be attached other than the Aboriginality of the titleholders; no requirements to run sheep or cattle or to perform any other activity to justify the allocation of the land. It should not be possible to sell this land.

6) Allied to greater awareness and improving attitudes about conservation, but at the same time pointing to the need for long-term national policies in this area, there are probably many areas where a system of joint tenure of national parks could be given to Aboriginal groups on the basis that the parks are then administered and serviced by national parks authorities and that there is no unreasonable exclusion of non-Aboriginals. This is happening in effect very successfully at Uluru National Park, despite the attempts of politicians to discredit things. The Bass Strait Islands are an excellent case in point. There are Aboriginal people who live on, use and care about these islands. In fact even the farming communities on these islands might be better served if there was a national park classification which did not affect their titles over their farms. Farmers are very effective custodians of national parks in the United Kingdom. There needs to be a total and unequivocal ban on mining in national parks; and thereafter the principle that parks are for people to use but not abuse is best demonstrated by a recognition that this is simply how the Aboriginals kept Australia beautiful for thousands of years. The promoters of tourism should be reminded that the aura of magnificent natural features like Uluru and Kakadu are best conveyed by reference to Aboriginal mythology and association.

Tourism is probably Australia's most important industry, and I am asked constantly, especially by international tourists, why they cannot see more of Aboriginal people and their culture. At the same time Aboriginal people, who often live in close proximity to national parks visited by tourists, are the most unemployed group in Australia. There are some people who would say that Aboriginals are unemployable. They should be dismissed with the rejoinder that Aboriginals were once the backbone of the Australian pastoral industry. It would be immoral for a responsible government to take the same attitude and the easy way out, paying unemployment benefits to the majority of Aboriginals forever. For unemployment is morale-shattering if nothing else. The problem for Aboriginals is that they have never been given proper motivation to work.

Perhaps a positive national project could be launched whereby major national parks were declared additionally as 'areas for the preservation of Aboriginal culture'. A meaningful long-term program of training Aboriginal people in all aspects of employment for the various Parks and Wildlife organisations, and in the various industries which support tourism — particularly the manufacture and sale of good quality artifacts — could be organised. There has been some commendable work in this field already, but the principal need is to promote public awareness of what is being planned and done, principally to alleviate concern among non-Aboriginals. It is necessary to stress that such declarations do not inhibit access to Reserves for non-Aboriginals. This is vital for areas like Katherine Gorge, where there is ongoing Aboriginal association with the area, but where anti-Aboriginal hysteria is whipped up any time the words 'land rights' are used.

There is no doubt that Aboriginals, men and women, are suited for employment relating to the preservation and development of national parks. Significantly the locations of the larger national parks coincide with the presence of those Aboriginal groups who still have meaningful retention of their traditional culture.

7) There are only two problems for Aboriginals in Australia. One relates to land, the other to identity. Those Aboriginals who, through no fault of their own, have lost their traditions should be given positive assistance to redevelop their identity. This is not to suggest that town dwellers should submit to initiation ceremonies totally foreign to them. But bad health, disastrous or inadequate diet, unsatisfactory housing, alcohol and drug abuse, inferior education and unemployment are all indicators of people so depressed, demoralised, dispossessed, frustrated and infuriated that they perhaps feel they have nothing more to lose. Inordinate sums of government money have been, and continue to be, virtually wasted, and these 'seeming problems' will only be overcome by improved morale and pride, and the preparedness of all Australians to tackle the real issues affecting Aboriginals.

8) Given positive programs in the land and identity areas — and this would involve governments saying what they will not do as much as what they will do — attempts should then be made to depoliticise the lives of Aboriginals as far as possible. Get rid of the cumbersome government agencies and the often ill-intentioned and devious people who run them. Stop throwing incredible sums of money around in pork-barrelling handouts which do not resolve problems but do promote corruption. Stop the more political Aboriginal groups from getting funding simply on the basis of their political contacts and cunning, and often to the detriment of other Aboriginals.

Sound policies, not inordinate sums of money, are what is needed in Australia. But that's asking for responsible government based on humanitarian principles.

'All I ask is a fair go…' (Photo by Allan Howard)

Prominent and Proud Aboriginals

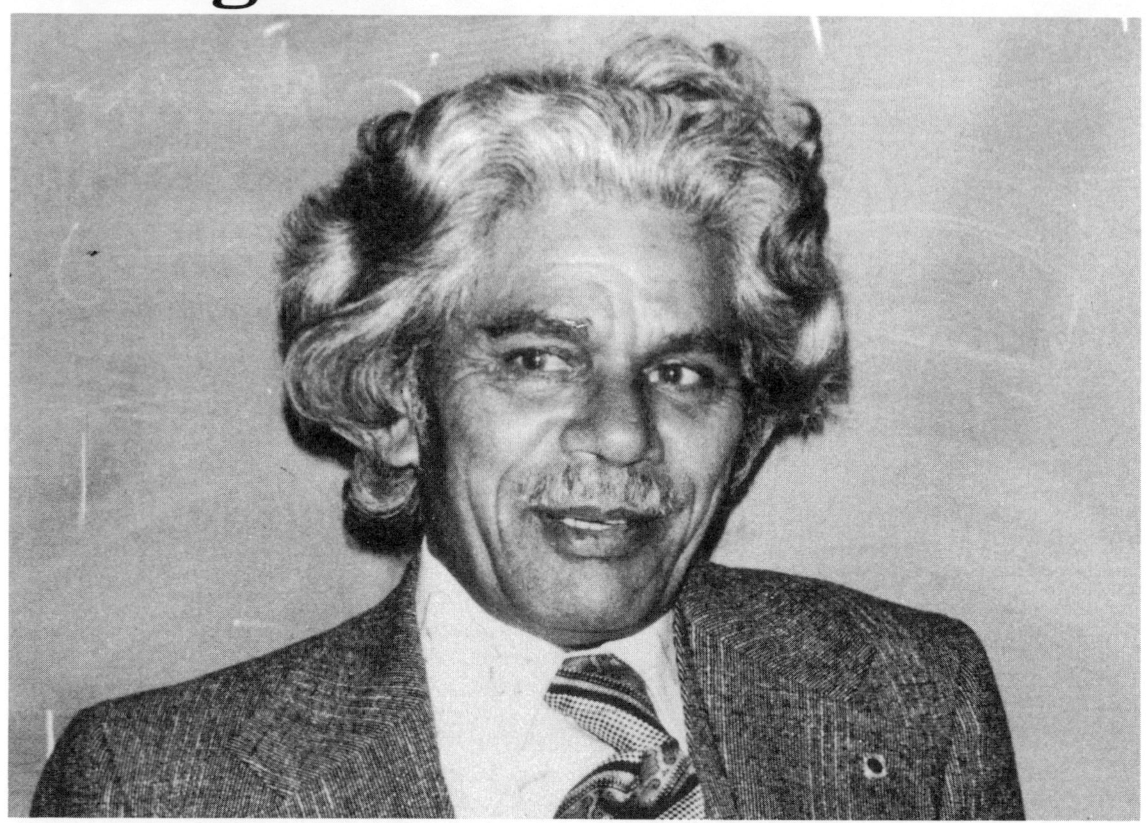

Senator Neville Bonner, first Aboriginal to enter Federal Parliament (Photo by Aleck Jackomos; Australian Institute of Aboriginal Studies)

Charles Perkins, first Aboriginal University Graduate, noted sportsman, first Aboriginal to become Permanent Head of a Commonwealth Department (Photo Department of Aboriginal Affairs)

David Gulpilil, magnificent dancer, star of many films, including Storm Boy, Walkabout and Mad Dog Morgan (Photo by Aleck Jackomos; Australian Institute of Aboriginal Studies)

Pat O'Shane, first Aboriginal barrister (Photo by Penny Tweedie; Australian Institute of Aboriginal Studies)

Jack Davis, famous playwright and poet (Photo Department of Aboriginal Affairs)

Kath Walker, poet and author (Photo by Aleck Jackomos; Australian Institute of Aboriginal Studies)

King Wally

Words and Music: Ernie Dingo

Country blues feel

Well, I heard this morning old King Wally
      has died
To the Dreamtime his soul is on its flight
Though I never knew the man
I was proud to shake his hand
As he'd bum me for a cigarette and a light.

People say he was a drunkard and a bum
But they just don't know the hard road that
      he'd come
He left his spear behind
The good life for to find
Just to find it full of pain and misery.

The reminder of the life our people knew
He used to walk the city streets without his shoes
And the spear he held so grand
Turned to a bottle in his hand
And he slept where all the ragged people go.

Now King Wally's gone, I hope he finds his peace
In the Dreamtime I pray his soul they'll keep
In my life he was just a passer-by
But that night I heard the lonely curlew cry.

Well I heard this morning old King Wally
      has died
To the Dreamtime his soul is on its flight
And the morning papers say
Last night he passed away
King Wally, do you hear a distant call?
King Wally, do you hear a different call?
King Wally, did you hear that distant call?

Bibliography and Recommended Reading

Gilbert, Kevin J.   *Living Black: Blacks Talk to Kevin Gilbert*, Allen Lane, Melbourne, 1978

Gilbert, Kevin J.   *People Are Legends: Aboriginal Poems by Kevin Gilbert*, University of Queensland Press, St Lucia, 1978

Perkins, Charles Nelson   *A Bastard Like Me*, Ure Smith, Sydney, 1975

Walker, Kath   *Father Sky and Mother Earth,* Jacaranda Wiley, Milton, 1985

Walker, Kath   *My People,* 2nd edition, Jacaranda Wiley, Milton, 1981

Wilmot, Eric   *Out of the Silent Land*, report of the Task Force on Aboriginal and Islander Broadcasting and Communications, AGPS, Canberra, 1984

TRADITIONAL LIFE

Amadio, N. (ed)   *Albert Namatjira*, Macmillan, Melbourne, 1986

Berndt, R.M. & C.H.   *The World of the First Australians*, Ure Smith, Sydney, 1964

Berndt, R.M. & C.H. (ed)   *Aboriginal Man in Australia*, Angus & Robertson, Sydney, 1965

Blainey, G.   *Triumph of the Nomads: A History of Ancient Australia*, Macmillan, Melbourne, 1975

Elkin, A.P.   *The Australian Aborigines*, Angus & Robertson, Sydney, 1938

Goodale, Jane   *Tiwi Wives; A Study of the women of Melville Island*, University of Washington Press, Seattle, 1971

Hiatt, Les   *Kinship and Conflict*, ANU Press, Canberra, 1965

Maddock, Kenneth   *The Australian Aborigines: A Portrait of their Society*, Penguin, 1972

Meggitt, M.   *Desert People,* Angus & Robertson, Sydney, 1962

Mulvaney, D.J.   *The Prehistory of Australia*, Thames & Hudson, London, 1979

Mulvaney, D.J. & Golson J. (ed)   *Aboriginal Man and Environment in Australia*, ANU Press, Canberra, 1971

Peterson, Nicolas   *Australian Territorial Organisation, Oceanic Monographs*, University of Sydney, 1986

Warner, Lloyd   *A Black Civilisation*, Harper & Row, New York, 1937, 1958

CONTACT AND CHANGE

Gale, Fay — *We are Bosses Ourselves: The Status and Role of Aboriginal Women Today*, AIAS, Canberra, 1986

Hercus, Louise & Sutton, Peter (eds) — *This is What Happened*, AIAS, Canberra, 1986

Long, Jeremy — *Aboriginal Settlements: A Survey of Institutional Communities in Eastern Australia*, ANU Press, Canberra, 1970

Reynolds, Henry — *The Other Side of the Frontier*, Melbourne, 1982

Rowley, Charles — *The Destruction of Aboriginal Society*, ANU Press, Canberra, 1970/Penguin, 1971.

Rowley, Charles — *The Remote Aborigines*, ANU Press, Canberra, 1980/Penguin, 1972

Rowley, Charles — *Outcasts in White Australia*, ANU Press, Canberra, 1970/Penguin, 1972

Tonkinson, Robert — *The Jigalong Mob: Aboriginal Victors of the Desert Crusade*, Cummings Publishing Company, California, 1974.

Tatz, Colin — *Aborigines and Uranium and Other Essays*, Heinemann, Melbourne, 1982.

Tatz, Colin — *Aborigines in Sport, Encyclopedia of the Australian People*, Australian Bicentennial Authority Publication, Canberra, 1987.

Guitar Chords

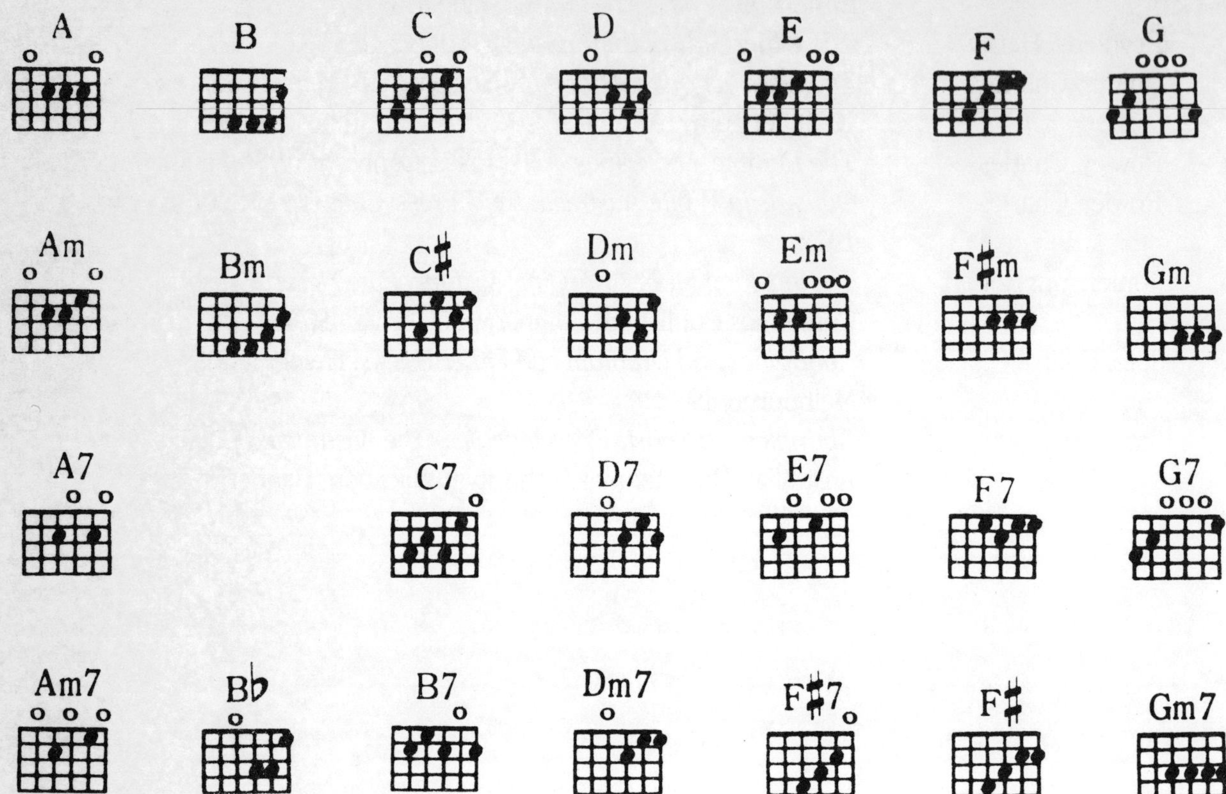